Farm, Forge and Factory

The life of a village one hundred years ago

Cliff Hardy

G000036854

Lavenham in 1929

© Cliff Hardy 1992
Published 1992 by Cliff Hardy, 8 High Street, Lavenham, Sudbury, Suffolk

ISBN 0 9519811 0 2

Design and composition by Sally Jeffery
Printed in England by The Lavenham Press

Front cover: Haymaking on a Lavenham farm
Back cover: Lady Street, Lavenham in the early years of the century

Contents

Lavenham rooftops

Acknowledgements

My thanks are due to the following for making this work possible: the Lavenham Guildhall Museum Committee for permission to reproduce photographs; the Baker family of Lavenham for permission to use extracts from the farming diary of John Woodgate Baker; Mr John C. Wolton of Little Saxham, Suffolk for his guidance and information about Lavenham Hall and the life of William Biddell JP MP; Mr C. V. F. Hawkins of Milden for permission to use extracts from a report of a meeting of the Lavenham Farmers' Club published in the *Suffolk and Essex Free Press* in April 1869, and extracts from an account rendered to Hill Farm in 1891; the late Mr Philip Fayers of Lavenham for information on farming practices in Lavenham, and for permission to use information contained in the farm notebooks of his father, Sam Fayers, bailiff to John Woodgate Baker; Miss Eileen Huffey for sharing her knowledge of the village and for telling me about her father; and Mrs Elsie Hynard for the vivid portrait she gave me of her father and his work.

Introduction

Life in rural England today stands in sharp contrast to life as it was lived in English villages one hundred years ago. There are many who regret the changes which have taken place and they hanker after a way of life once commonplace in English rural society, when lifestyles were simple and the pace much slower. Such belief is misplaced and is borne out of a misunderstanding or is the result of an over-romantic view of life in the country. It is a refusal to accept the facts of life as they really were.

This is not to deny that men and women in English villages a hundred years ago lived more wholesome lives and embraced a set of values which are missing today. At the same time life was often a struggle for survival and contained much hardship. What marks it out from an urban existence is that it was a life lived close to the natural environment and one which people took a hand in shaping. Most men and their families were involved in the production of crops and the care of livestock or were in occupations closely related to the life of the farms.

When the farmworker looked out of his cottage door in the morning and observed the weather and the signs of weather to come (a skill developed from his own observations over a long period) he did so with one purpose: how would he be occupied that day? Would it be fine enough to carry on with the harvest? Would it be too wet to plough? Would it keep fine long enough to carry the remainder of the hay in Baggs Meadow? (Not all questions for one day, of course.) He cared about this, it was not just another day at work wishing that Sunday would soon come. His work and its demands were all-pervading and the weather played a critical part.

Despite all the difficulties – hard work, low pay – there was a sense of harmony between the man and his work. There was a sense of pride in a job well done and he could measure the results for himself. He also knew that a lot of other people would see the results. Sometimes he would look critically at his efforts with a view to improving his performance the next time round.

Although in many villages the composition of the population has changed, and many people have come from urban backgrounds, the essential core remains intact and is recognizable. The basic elements and some of the traditional buildings remain almost as they were when first built. There is also an almost universal desire to preserve things as they are or as they used to be. Any proposal to knock anything down these days is met with a firm rejection, and as a result rural England is much admired by visitors and natives alike.

The same passion for preservation applies to the landscape around our villages, although where urban development has taken control the landscape has been wiped out; a matter for regret but in many ways inevitable in the face of pressure for more housing.

In contrast to a hundred years ago the people who now live in villages and work on farms within the parish can be counted on the fingers of one hand. This is not to say that villagers engaged in other occupations are indifferent to the agricultural industry by which they are surrounded: they generally take a keen interest in what happens on the farms. The farmer is generally rated highly by those who have settled in villages, although they may get a little irate when, for instance, straw burning is taking place. Fortunately this practice is much reduced as the result of legislation, in which the National Farmer's Union was able to bring some influence to bear. Not being able to burn created problems for the farmer which the layman found difficult to understand.

The desire to get near to the land is deep-rooted in the population, for how else can we explain the strong desire in people to leave the towns and cities and take up residence in the countryside? Amongst them are some who hold strong views about the need to return to a more natural way of life. This often means getting closer to the soil.

All of the foregoing is true of Lavenham, a mediaeval village in the heart of Suffolk, famous for its wealth of well-preserved mediaeval buildings, its guildhall and its church. It is famous too for its involvement in the spinning of wool, in the making of wool cloth (Lavenham Serge) and later the making of coconut matting and horsehair fabric, and it is unique in that these crafts and industries grew and prospered alongside its extensive farming scene. Many of the crafts supporting the farming sector were available to other industries as they developed – the blacksmith being a typical example.

The village went through times of prosperity not known in many places. Many of the cottages would have had their own looms, and later the small factories provided work for the girls and women of the village. A number of men were also employed on the heavy tasks within the factories.

A hundred and more years ago agriculture was the main source of employment for the men of the village and at one time as many as 300 people were involved, some indirectly as blacksmiths, saddlers and other craftsmen (today the numbers involved would be fewer than twenty, some of whom are owner occupiers of the farms). This book seeks to demonstrate the all-embracing influence of farming in Lavenham then, on the lives of the people involved in it, and its impact on other people in the village who were not directly concerned. It is a portrait of Lavenham as it used to be.

The period was not one of great change but it was a prelude to what turned out to be a revolution – brought about by the introduction of tractors into the industry and all that flowed from this application of power and rapid mechanization. It would be an error to regard the days before mechanization as an idyllic time in which to have lived. It was a hard and sometimes harsh environment. Organic farming was practised for there was no alternative and crops were grown without help from chemical sprays and artificial fertilizers. Horses provided motive power, relieving some of the burden of human effort, and leaving the air unpolluted by noxious fumes.

Some workers had 'free accommodation' in the farmer's property and benefited from a garden or strip of land on which to grow their own vegetables. On the other hand wages were low and losing a job may well have led to the loss of a home. The farmers had their own problems trying to make a living in a period frequently affected by economic depression. They needed strength of character and considerable skill to survive in such times. We are bound to stand in some awe at the way people coped with such problems, working as they often did twelve hours a day for six days a week with very limited holidays.

These times are reflected in this book. They are not recorded in an attempt to apportion blame, but only to 'tell it as it was'. What comes through is that we are looking at a breed of men who believed strongly in the importance of their daily work and to the best of their ability carried it out to a high standard. Many worked daily with horses. Everything they did called for skill and stamina of the highest order, and an innate wisdom and knowledge the like of which we shall not see again. It was a way of life that cannot be repeated, even if we wished it to be so.

1 Lavenham today

Drive into Lavenham on any Sunday in the summer or even some-times in the winter and you will find the High Street, the Market Place and Water Street full of visitors. You will see them gaze with some wonder at the timber buildings with which the place abounds. The Crooked House (see below) in the High Street is probably the most frequently photographed building in any English village. It is a fine example of a mediaeval timber house – but it is marked out because it leans drunkenly on the neighbouring property, the Old Post Office, and appears to be parting company with No. 8 High Street, the pink cottage on its left. Local people will tell you that it will not move any further as it has now 'settled'. Credibility is given to this when you are informed that it has stood there almost unchanged since it was built in about 1300. Seven hundred years is a fair test for the truth of this assertion.

Going back over the years we learn that two of these three proper-ties have been used for purposes other than the original one as

The Crooked House (leaded windows) in the High Street

dwellings. The Old Post Office is self-explanatory, and No. 8 has been used as a general store, a cobbler's shop and a sweet shop. This kind of history is echoed in many of the dwellings in the village for at one period there were over forty premises being used as shops.

Should you be in need of refreshment you could visit one of a number of restaurants and teashops, or one of the four licensed premises: the Swan, the Old Cock, the Greyhound and the Angel. These are likely to be serving food and beer to the visitors, and amongst the visitors you will find a sprinkling of Lavenham people, but they will be in a minority. A hundred years ago the inhabitants of Lavenham and surrounding areas had the choice of nine public houses. Visitors from further afield would be a rare sight except on special occasions, such as a fair. In addition to the four above the other five were the Black Lion (in the High Street), the Three Blackbirds (Market Lane), the White Horse (Water Street), the Anchor (Prentice Street) and the One

Market Lane as it once was. The Great House can be seen across the Market Place.

Bell (High Street). These buildings remain intact and are now used as dwellings (some divided into several dwellings). The original names still appear on what were the Three Blackbirds and the White Horse.

The church

A big attraction to the tourist is the magnificent Parish Church of St Peter and St Paul, which is in the diocese of St Edmundsbury. It is a large and commanding building, typical of many such churches in Suffolk which were built using money donated by families who had prospered from their involvement in the wool and wool cloth making trades. Fortunately for Lavenham one such merchant lived in the village – a Thomas Spring, who lavished much of his wealth on extending and improving the existing church.

A hundred years ago this church played a dominant role in the life of the people, particularly of those engaged in the production of food from the land. Many of the festivals and special days had their origins in the cycle of production from the soil.

New Year's Day was the first of these, when a watch night service would be held in the church to see the death of December and the birth of January. The bells would be rung to herald the new year and in the cottages toasts would be drunk in home-made wine. Blessings would be sought for the people of the village and for the beasts and crops of the farms.

Twelfth Night (then called the Feast of the Epiphany) was the next celebration, and singing would be heard coming from the lighted windows of the cottages where people got together to celebrate the second milestone of the year. The main drink, called Wassail, was a very strong concoction of ale, roasted apples, sugar, nutmeg and toast.

Not many days after this event came Plough Monday when the priest was asked to bless the plough. On the previous day a plough would have been taken into the church supported by the men and women from the farms. The significance of this was that it was the first working day on the land after Christmas, and it marked the beginning of the farming year. On Rogation Sunday the farming community would ask the priest to go out into the fields with his cross bearers and choir. They would process round the parish boundary going into as many fields as possible seeking a blessing on crops and animals, that they would yield well.

The culmination of this close association between the church and the farms was the Harvest Festival, when all the village would gather in the church and give thanks to God for his bountiful gifts of food. The Harvest Festival in Lavenham church is a great celebration still.

The Church and the Salvation Army play an important part in the life of Lavenham today, but the relationship between farming and the Church does not stand out in such high relief as it did a hundred years ago simply because the number of people involved in farming is now so small. The church has always dominated the landscape in Lavenham and that has not changed, for from almost any point within the parish a view of the church can be seen. It stands as a commanding landmark over the village, at night like a beacon for it is permanently floodlit; a reminder to all that man does not live by bread alone and should aspire to a more spiritual order. Our forefathers felt that there were times when they needed to give thanks, and times when they needed help. The Church supplied this need.

The evolving streetscape

The landscape of the parish of Lavenham has changed little over the last one hundred and fifty years. In one or two places small plots of land have been used for house building and one small factory has been built. A sensible balance has been struck between private and public housing. In the streets the policy has been to ensure a balance between domestic properties and those used for trade. Credit must be given to the planning committee of the District Council and its officers for their vigilance. Lavenham has been well preserved to the benefit of posterity. Long may it remain so.

In the original part of the village some minor changes have taken place along the streets. In the period during which the coconut matting industry and rope and horsehair manufacture flourished, more houses were needed to accommodate some of the workers. These houses (about 50 of them) are spread throughout the village and are easily recognized by their character, totally different from the earlier ones. They are built in the main of red or white brick, some in terraces, others semi-detatched.

The major changes have been brought about by renovation, but it is very closely controlled by the local authority. Some 70 per cent of Lavenham properties are protected and the result is that owners have

Little Hall, with the Great House to the left

done their utmost to preserve them in a condition as near to the original as possible. Another big change in the character of the village is the type and number of shops. In 1880 there were over forty shops in Lavenham to serve 1,800 people. They were clearly needed at this time when the village had to be self-sufficient, and means of transport were limited. Today the community is well served by essential shops: two grocers, a bakery, a greengrocer, a butcher, a newsagent, a flower shop, a draper and outfitter's, three dress shops and two hairdressers, along with a sub-post office and a chemist's shop. In addition there are a number of gift shops providing merchandise for visitors. It would still be true to say that Lavenham can supply most ordinary human needs.

Apart from the church, three substantial buildings are open to the public. These are the Guildhall, Little Hall and the Priory. All are of considerable historical and architectural importance. The Guildhall houses a museum of Lavenham life, and has a fascinating history. Little Hall is a fine timber-framed building dating back to the fourteenth century. It now houses the offices of the Suffolk Preservation Society. Most of the restoration was carried out by the Gayer-Anderson brothers. They were twins born in 1881 and both had army careers. They bequeathed the house to Surrey County Coucil for use as a hostel for art students. It was offered to the Suffolk Building Preservation Trust in 1974. The Priory, an old timbered house of immense interest, was once occupied by the rector of the parish, then became a farmhouse, and has now been carefully restored by its present owners, Mr and Mrs Casey.

Lavenham boasts a market place, and market day was on a Tuesday. At one stage it was a place where much meat was sold, but records of its more recent use are hard to find. There is reference in early wills to stall holders' rights being passed on, but it seems that it ceased to be used as a conventional market place in 1775. Until 1922 it was the site of Lavenham's annual fair which took place on Shrove Tuesday, no doubt part of the original Horse Fair.Today the Market Place would be regarded as the hub of the village, dominated by the Guildhall with its own National Trust shop and tearoom. It is enclosed on the east side by the Angel Hotel, the Great House Restaurant and Little Hall, on the north side by Heeks grocer's shop, Faiers and Sparlings bakery and the Book and Kettle bookshop, and on the west side by Miss Ranson's outfitter's shop, all interspersed with dwellings of various shapes and sizes.

The big open centre of the Market Place serves as a car park. When this is full, as it frequently is, the full impact of the view is obscured. To get the best impression it should be seen early on a bright morning before the activities of the day begin, or on a quiet summer evening when all the cars have gone. Only then will its uniqueness be revealed. To stand then in the centre of the Market Place and observe the wonderful mixture of roofs and chimneys overtopping buildings of great charm is an experience not to be missed. Nothing offends the eye and the viewer could almost believe he or she had been transported back a hundred years. Apart from some demolition in the centre of the open space, little has changed. Many villages developed round an open space or clearing, which we now know as the village green. Lavenham has no such green but there is a common on the eastern outskirts of the village. It is likely that the vicinity of the Swan Hotel was the place where people first settled and started to build.

Leading from the square one finds streets full of houses and cottages following the same pattern. It would be safe to say that you will not find a duplicate in any of these streets save for one or two red-brick houses built at the end of the nineteenth century. The same can be said of High Street, Church Street and Water Street. The High Street, just off the Market Place, where the village was first established, would have been on the main highway from Sudbury to Bury St Edmunds.

The main appeal of Lavenham to visitors and to its residents is its large collection of ancient buildings in such a wonderful state of preservation. Many of them are even more interesting on the inside, with their wealth of exposed timbers and unusually-shaped rooms, built by craftsmen in the style known as the vernacular. Lavenham has been described as one of the finest examples of a medieval village in England. Much of the credit for the state of preservation now found in the village must go to people like Mr Francis Lingard Ranson, village tailor and keen historian. He became concerned about the decay and dereliction which had been wrought on the buildings during periods of depression. The troughs of depression which took hold of the agricultural industry a century ago were reflected in the village. Many of those employed on the surrounding farms lived in the village itself, and the concentration of poverty was acute. In the 1940s Mr Ranson sought to raise public awareness of the problem of decay and the need to try and change the trend towards preservation. His and others' efforts led to the formation of the Suffolk Preservation Society, of which he became the first Vice-President. He also published an authoritative history of Lavenham.

Cottages opposite the church, fallen into dereliction. They are now a tea-shop.

The view from the church tower

The surrounding countryside

There is more to Lavenham than the village itself, for it is placed in gently undulating countryside criss-crossed by bridleways and footpaths which are well maintained. It is an ideal spot for those who like to walk and see another aspect of the life of a village. You will find such walks take you across some of the best-farmed land in Suffolk, with well-kept hedgerows and roadways. You will also find that you can even walk most of the lanes in comparative safety for traffic is light except on the main road from Bury to Sudbury which passes through the centre of the village. A map of the footpaths is available in some of the shops.

Looking at Lavenham today it seems unlikely that any further significant changes will take place; even the redundant mills have been saved. Two have been restored, not to their original uses as places for manufacture, but for use as dwellings. I think their conversion into places where people now live does great credit to the architects concerned. In Ropers Court and Bakers Mill we see an enlightened approach to redevelopment: not to sweep the old away but to let it be and bring it into use as places where people can live and take their place in the life of the village community. In the following chapters we will look back to a period over a hundred years ago and try to discover what life was like in Lavenham and in the countryside around – for at that time there was an indispensable link between the two.

2 The land and its people

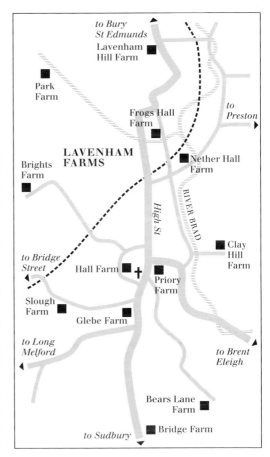

to Bury
St Edmunds

Lavenham
Hill Farm

Park
Farm

Frogs Hall
Farm

to
Preston

**LAVENHAM
FARMS**

Brights
Farm

Nether Hall
Farm

High St

RIVER BRAD

Clay
Hill
Farm

to Bridge
Street

Hall Farm

Priory
Farm

Slough
Farm

Glebe Farm

to Long
Melford

to Brent
Eleigh

Bears Lane
Farm

to Sudbury

Bridge Farm

Although the shape, the size, and the layout of most of the farms in the parish of Lavenham have hardly changed in a century, the land has changed hands many times, and has been subjected to a whole range of management styles. The system of landlord and tenant was common a hundred years ago and tenancies changed frequently. Today the system has almost gone and most of the farms are owner-occupied. Only three of the 11 farms are no longer operating as separate units: Priory, Glebe and Brights. Their land is now owned and farmed by neighbouring farmers and although the Priory and Brights farmhouses still stand, the Glebe farmhouse has long since been demolished.

In 1880 the farms ringed the residential part of the village, and in some cases, the land abutted on to the back gardens of the houses and cottages. In this respect and many others the farms and the village were closely integrated. Several farmhouses were within a few yards of the village streets, and from the streets and houses could be heard the familiar sounds of the farmyard activities. This was true of Netherhall, the Priory, the Glebe and to some extent Lavenham Hall.

The two largest farms, Park Farm and Hill Farm, had cottages situated near to the farm buildings which were occupied by key workers

*Archie Wells
of the
Cock Inn
supplements
his income*

such as horsemen and cattlemen, but in most other cases the workers lived in cottages in the village, some of which were owned or rented by their employers.

In addition to these eleven farms there were some smaller parcels of land bordering on the village which were used by individuals for keeping a few cattle, pigs and poultry. Such pieces of land would often run from the back of the house. In other cases the owners or tenants would have a small yard and buildings on one of the streets quite some distance from the land they farmed.

Farming methods

Within the parish boundary the soil varies from very heavy loam over clay to light loam over gravel. Most farms have some flat land, but many have the benefit of a gentle slope which assists the drainage systems. The river Brad or Brett runs in the valley which is east of the village and in which can be found fertile water meadows.

Overall the land is very fertile and even in the days of horses it was in the main reasonably easy to work. These were days when farmers needed to 'walk' their land regularly to see the changes taking place, mainly influenced by the weather. 'You had', the farmers would say, 'to catch it right'. There was a right time and a wrong time for horses, men and implements to be on the land, and it was at this point that the farmer's judgement was critical.

Farming in Lavenham as anywhere else was influenced by periods of depression, but the evidence shows that even in bad times a good standard of husbandry was practised, for it was a golden rule in farming that the level of fertility had to be maintained in order to ensure that those coming after took over the land in 'good heart'.

The biggest contrast between today and a hundred years ago is in the type of system practised by the farmers. Today the crops are limited to cereals, sugar beet, oil seed rape and some beans, with only small numbers of livestock kept (although on one or two farms numbers have increased in recent years), whereas a hundred years ago the farmers practised a most comprehensive system of mixed farming. The fertility of the farm was maintained by keeping relatively large numbers of livestock, such as fattening cattle, sheep and in some cases milking cows. Most of the land was under the plough, although most farms kept a small amount of permanent meadowland. Clover and ryegrass leys were sown for cutting as hay for the livestock including the horses, and these were part of the cropping plan which was so important. It was regarded as almost a sin to ignore a proper crop rotation.

Today's systems would have been regard by farmers a hundred years ago as madness, leading in due course to the ruin of the land, for there is little or no rotation of crops, and farmyard manure is not regarded as important to the health of the soil. Things are beginning to change, however, and farmers are being encouraged to adopt organic methods.

Although today's systems on Lavenham farms are far removed from 1880, nonetheless the standards of husbandry in the parish are very high. Hedges and ditches are probably as tidy today as ever they were and crop yields are invariably high. In 1880 an average yield of wheat would have been about one ton per acre, whilst today it is likely to be about three tons per acre. Capital investment is very high both in machinery and in buildings which are designed for maximum efficiency.

It would be hard to find an industry today which has lifted its productivity at the same rate as British agriculture. In some respects this has been to its disadvantage, for the problem now is one of over production of many commodities. This is not true of course if one takes a global view, where we find large numbers of people living at starvation level, and although some of the crops we produce could not be used in other parts of the world there is no doubt that grain would always be acceptable.

Changing fortunes

Farmers in 1880 were far from inefficient. They had to be good managers or they would not have survived in a most difficult economic climate. In 1860 British farming was enjoying a period of expansion as the population grew rapidly and the demand for food grew as a consequence, but from 1875 onwards two factors brought about a reversal in the situation. Large amounts of cheap food were flooding into the country and at the same time four years of bad weather reduced the yield from British farms. Prices of home grown food fell as did the amount available for sale, a disastrous situation for producers.

By 1880 things had deteriorated, and Lavenham did not escape the effects of the depression which had overtaken the industry. The average wage of a farm worker then was fifteen shillings per week (75p). Fortunately for the people of Lavenham, the position was somewhat alleviated by the fact that horsehair weaving and coconut matting manufacture were now well-established in the village. These two industries provided employment for about 200 women (in horsehair) and 40 men in matting making.

Most families were large but with some members finding employment in these two industries extreme poverty was kept at bay for many of them. In some cases wives went out to work as weavers in Roper's factories and some 40 were there in 1881. In addition a total of 102 sons and daughters of Lavenham families also worked in horsehair manufacture as did some 16 men of the village. It is of interest to note that these men were fathers of children who were also in horsehair. They could well have come into the village to work specifically for Ropers, as they occupied houses which were built by the manufacturer.

Married couples in Lavenham then had an average of four children, but quite a number had five and several up to nine. It was common to find mother and father and five or six children living in cottages which were really only large enough to accommodate parents and one child. There were obviously many cases of gross overcrowding.

There was a limited number of houses with the luxury of piped water and indoor sanitation. Water had to be carried either from a pump in the street or taken from a well in the garden, most of which have since been filled in, some of them only in recent years. Mains water came to the village in 1936.

Many of the gardens at the back of the cottages still have buildings remaining which used to contained the sanitation bucket. These were aspects of village life which we would find hard to tolerate today, and were far from the idyllic picture we tend to conjure up of life in the country. When snow lay thick on the ground and temperatures were

Carrying water,
Church Street

well below freezing and darkness had fallen, the old and young had no option but to trudge many yards down the garden path to the privy, where perhaps a small oil lantern or a candle burned to lighten the gloom. In some more advanced communities a horse-drawn cart would call at the cottages in the village and carry away the contents of the privy bucket. It was often an activity undertaken at night for obvious reasons.

Because many of the farms were on the edge of Lavenham the journey for the agricultural worker to his place of work was an easy one. Only in the case of Park, Hill and Brights farms was much travelling involved. In these cases well-worn footpaths and bridleways were used, leading in an almost straight line from the village to the farms. Such daily travel was often the reason why footpaths were established.

The footpaths we walk today in and around Lavenham, mainly for pleasure, were established for a more serious purpose. They took the shortest line to the farms or to neighbouring villages, such as Preston St Mary, Brent Eleigh, Waldingfield, Acton and Long Melford. The most popular one in use today follows the old railway track from Lavenham to Long Melford, and along its length much evidence exists that it was once owned and operated by the Great Eastern Railway Company, linking Long Melford with Bury St Edmunds.

The workers on the farms

We know that in 1881 there were 206 agricultural workers living within the parish boundary, the majority in the village itself, and we know roughly how many were employed on each of the farms. At Park Farm (500 acres) twenty men and ten boys were at work, and at Hill Farm (478 acres) where George Mumford's widow Annie Mumford lived, the record shows that 20 men and 20 boys were employed. Benjamin Bantock, who was landlord of the Angel Hotel in Market Place, farmed 100 acres in various parts of the parish and employed five men and two boys on his land. Lavenham Hall, owned and farmed by William Biddell, employed 24 men and 11 boys. The farm was about 250 acres, and about this time Mr Biddell also acquired the Priory, Glebe and Frogs Hall farms. At Netherhall Farm, owned by Mr J. T. Cousens, five men were employed, and at Frogs, farmed by John Allen, five men and three boys were at work.

Building a hay stack with a team of five. In front is Violet Knights.

Sir William Hyde Parker of Melford Hall (over the parish boundary) owned a large estate and one of the farms, Slough, of 240 acres, was tenanted by George Pulford with 10 men employed there in 1881. Most of the farm fell within the parish boundary. The Glebe Farm, at one time owned by the rector by virtue of his office, employed four or five men. At Bridge Farm another five men would have been at work. At Lodge Farm Mr Patte employed four men and three boys, and at Priory Farm William Making employed eight men and three boys on 171 acres. In 1889 Thomas Baker bought the 192-acre Brights Farm and would have employed some eight or ten men.

Most of the figures given are authenticated by the census returns of 1881, but some gaps do appear. It is not possible to reconcile all the figures exactly, and some of the workers recorded would be employed on a casual basis to meet the demands of the season. The significant information is that most of the agricultural workers in Lavenham at this time would be working on Lavenham farms. The permanent men were highly skilled and would work the horses but the most highly skilled of all would be the ploughmen. No farmworker could have been classified as unskilled, for any task, however lowly, demanded its own level of skill. With the large number of agricultural workers available, the competition for employment was strong and it follows that the men with the widest range of skills would be selected.

Farmers and landowners

As already mentioned some of the tenancies of the farms in the parish from 1880 onwards changed hands frequently. Times were bad and it was not easy to make a living from farming; landlords often had difficulty in finding tenants who were prepared to take the risks involved. Some of them, despite working hard, were forced to relinquish their tenancies in order to avoid insolvency.

From 1850 to 1889 Brights Farm, of 102 acres, changed hands several times until it was bought by Thomas Baker, farmer and miller, of Prentice Street, from which time the farm prospered. When Mr Baker died in 1892 the farm was left to his family and was managed by one of the sons, John Woodgate Baker, on their behalf. In 1913 he bought the farm at auction and continued to farm it with a high degree of expertise until he died in 1933.

During his association with the farm over a period of thirty years John Woodgate Baker meticulously kept a farm diary.* This diary contains a wealth of information about his own management of the farm, but in addition his comments on farming in general and the economic situation in agriculture are very informative. He was also farming at Netherhall and in the neighbouring village of Milden.

The first diary entry was for 4th November 1903, and in essence it is a most valuable and authentic account of farming practices in Lavenham between 1900 and 1927. It records so many important facts, such as the weather, details of what was being undertaken on the farms at any particular time – seeding rates, crop yields, prices of seed and prices of the commodities and livestock going off the farm. It is a unique document, written by a man of great character and understanding, and in addition the technical information demonstrates a high quality of farm management. Frequent reference to his

*John Woodgate Baker, diaries (Lavenham Guildhall Museum).

diary is made throughout this book as it provides a most valuable background to much of the subject matter.

One of the most influential landowners and farmers was William Biddell MP JP, who lived and farmed at Lavenham Hall. The Hall and the farm buildings which surround it are more or less as they were in Mr Biddell's time. One or two necessary renovations have taken place, and some new buildings have been erected to meet additional needs, but the original character remains intact.

Lavenham Hall itself is a house of some distinction and set in landscaped gardens sweeping down to a substantial pond, now and possibly for a hundred years populated by mallard much loved by visitors and their children. It is situated at the end of Hall Road and can be seen from the footpath which runs from Hall Road to the churchyard. It is one of the prettiest corners of Lavenham, and a favourite walk for people of the village. The story of Lavenham Hall and the people who occupied it is a fascinating one. It was without doubt a place of considerable importance not only to Lavenham but over a much wider area.

The two largest farms in 1880 were Park Farm (500 acres) and Hill Farm (470 acres). They are set on the brow of the gentle slope which rises from the village going towards Bury St Edmunds and adjoin each other in two well-defined blocks of land. Together they account for one third of the agricultural land lying within the parish boundary.

In the mid 1880s Park Farm was in the ownership of Sir Isaac Strutt, a nationally-known name in farming circles. As a family they were involved in land management and in the application of scientific principles to agriculture. By 1881, the tenancy had passed into the hands of Edward Hitchcock, a young man with a small family, and a son of Thomas Hitchcock who was a corn merchant and farmer living in Prentice Street in the village. Edward kept a cook, a nurse and a governess – clearly a man of means.

In 1870 the owner of Hill Farm was George Mumford, a highly respected member of the farming community and one-time chairman of the Lavenham Farmers' Club. By 1881 Mr Mumford had died leaving a widow, Abigail, who continued to occupy the farm with her family. The farm was then being run by a group of executors. A farm bailiff, William Smith, was in post and would have been responsible for the day-to-day running of the farm.

John Allen was tenant at the 100-acre Frogs Hall Farm which was owned by Samuel Meeking, before it was purchased by William Biddell in 1899. John Allen was a farmer and seed grower and this suggests that he was an expert in this field, for only the best farmers were accepted as seed growers.

Netherhall Farm, of 129 acres, was in the ownership of John Cousens and was being managed by a farm bailiff, George Smith.

Lavenham's main dairy farm at this time was Priory Farm in Water Street. It had changed hands a few times in the mid 1800s but in 1880 it was occupied by William Making. The farm had a tradition for producing milk and had an acreage of permanent pasture above the average for Lavenham farms. Milk was being produced there in 1920 and for many years after. In the late 1880s the farm was bought by William Biddell and in 1896 the tenant was Charles Worter.

The Glebe Farm was in the gift of the Masters of Caius College, Cambridge and held by the rector, the Reverend Thomas Scott, in 1891. It was bought some time later by William Biddell.

Slough Farm, too, was occupied by a tenant. In 1881 a shepherd by the name of William Rouse occupied the farmhouse. In 1891 the tenant was George Pulford and in 1919 the tenancy was taken over by Bertram Death who was farming at Balsdon Hall just over the parish boundary. In due course Mr Death purchased the 230-acre farm from Sir William Hyde Parker, since which time it has been in the possession of the Death family.

In 1990 the land within the parish boundary is almost all owner-occupied. Whitton (Snarford) Farms Limited are at Lavenham Hall and take in the land that was once Brights Farm. Mr Philip Death owns Slough Farm. Frogs Hall is owned and farmed by Mr G. D. Norman, Netherhall by Mr N. J. Lane, Park Farm by Mr D. H. Holland. Hill Farm is owned and farmed by Mr H. J. Chrystal. Mr Geoffrey Fayers farms Bridge Farm on the Sudbury Road, and Bears Farm was taken over by Hill Farm, Brent Eleigh.

Over the past one hundred years the land stands out as the one constant factor in the working life of the village. The continuous relationship between the land and the people of Lavenham, and the gradual divorce of the two, is discussed in the following chapters.

3 An independent community

Although there is a sense of independence amongst the people of Lavenham today, a hundred years ago it was a dominant feature of the life of a village which did not have to rely on outsiders for its survival. Most requirements and services were obtainable within the village, apart from some raw materials such as coal, oil, horsehair and coconut fibre.

Craftsmen

A later chapter tells of the importance of the horse in Lavenham a century ago and this inevitably leads us to consider the work of the blacksmith, who spent much of his time providing a service to ensure the efficiency of the horse in particular and the farmer in general. In 1880 there were eleven skilled blacksmiths at work in the village, and forges were known to have existed in High Street (on the site presently occupied by the Co-op stores) and in Water Street (part of which premises are now used as a bookshop).

In 1898 Fred Huffey took over the Water Street premises, which were designed as a forge. He carried on his business there until the early forties. With his two sons he built a reputation for high quality work and was much sought after by farmers and others. Mr Huffey was a highly respected and well-liked member of the community. Water Street would see the daily passage of horses to the forge for the fitting of new shoes or for attention to a troublesome shoe. As winter approached and the first frost arrived, there would be a long queue of horses in Water Street waiting for frost nails to be fitted. Mr Huffey and his staff would also visit the farms to undertake some repair job that could not be brought to the forge. He would also make and supply a number of items for the farms, and an account dated 26th February 1898 shows that two new harrows were supplied to Hill Farm at a total cost of £1 12s od.

At about the same time the blacksmith in the High Street, John Wel-

From John Welton's blacksmith's account   Fred Huffey, blacksmith

ton, sent an account to Hill Farm (G. Mumford) containing 74 separate items and including work undertaken.* The 74 items in this
account tell us a great deal about what was going on at Hill Farm at
this time. We know that sheep were kept on the farm because Mr Welton supplied a Sheep Brand No. at 3d. The last item reads: 'Shoeing 10
Horses ¼ year ending Sep 30th/91 £1 10s 0d'. This indicates that there
were probably 20 or more horses at work on the farm in addition to a
number of young horses being 'broken in' ready for work. Other items
include '4 Shoes for young horse, and 4 Shoes for Colt'.

The blacksmith, of course, provided a service to other people in the
village apart from farmers. A few people had their own horses, a pony
or a cob, and there was a livery stable in Water Street owned by a Mr
Rudd. Additionally various tradesmen owned horses for transporting
merchandise. There were a coal dealer and three bakers, some of
whom would deliver in the village and surrounding areas. The corn
mill had its own transport as also did the railway; all of them would
be calling on the help of the blacksmith from time to time.

With the horse so important, the saddler and harness maker played

*Account rendered by Jno. Welton, 1891 (on loan to Lavenham Guildhall Museum).

The saddler's shop

a prominent role. A Mr Bullivant occupied a prominent position as the master saddler for many years, and trained and employed several skilled harness makers. His premises still stand, almost unchanged, in the High Street near the Greyhound Inn. The building still carries the name 'Saddlers'.

The saddler was to the horse what the tailor was to man. Collars and saddles had to be made to fit specific horses – there was little chance of an 'off the peg' collar fitting any horse. An ill-fitting collar or saddle would quickly give rise to sores, rendering the horse quite unfit for work for several days, until the sore had properly healed. The saddler would also make other leather goods such as bags and cases. An apprenticeship in saddlery and harness-making lasted five years – an indication of the high level of skill involved.

Waggons and carts were also made in the village by the wheelwright, and the main base for this was in Church Street, not far from the Water Street and Church Street crossroads. The premises are now dwellings and carry the name of 'Old Wheelwrights'. During the period covered, two names are associated with these premises: in the early part of the period James and Alfred Hoggar ran the business until it was taken over by Mr B. Deacon.

Including all the farm waggons and carts, and drays and carts owned by other tradespeople, there would have been 50 or 60 horse-drawn vehicles in and around the village in the late 19th century and a proportion of these would have been made in Church Street. However, the total demand could not have been met within the village and we learn from accounts that some were made by David Ward of Long Melford, who was also an ironfounder. A Thomas Bantock of Cockfield was also involved in supplying to farms.

The wheelwright's craft demanded many skills. He designed and built the body of the cart which called on all his skills in carpentry and wood turning. He made the wheels from many pieces of timber, assembled so that the rim was a true circle and the hub its true centre. The final operation was the fitting of the iron rim, which was done by the blacksmith in Lavenham for it required the use of a forge. One or two people in Lavenham today can remember seeing workmen from the wheelwright's shop rolling the new wheel down Water Street on their way to Mr Huffey's forge. It was customary for these waggons and carts to be decorated and turned out in bright shiny colours and this, of course, was almost akin to the skills of an artist.

Most of the wheelwright's time would be taken up with running repairs to existing vehicles. They were subject to hard wear and tear for the streets and roads were not surfaced with smooth tarmacadam, but were in some cases topped with cobble stones, and the farm roads with hard-core.

Provisions

No one needed to travel out of Lavenham to satisfy their needs. There were butchers, grocers, and general dealers, ironmongers, clothiers, boot and shoe makers and repairers. There were even a chemist and a hairdresser, a post office and a fishmonger. A straw bonnet maker found plenty of trade in the village, along with a watch maker and, most surprisingly, a marine store dealer. One can wonder how such a landlocked place could support a marine store dealer. It would have been difficult to find a village of the size of Lavenham which had so many shops available, including five butchers' shops, to supply a population of 1,800 people.

The mill owned by the Baker family would supply flour to at least two bakehouses in the village. The butchers would be taking pigs, cat-

tle and sheep from the farms around, probably supplied through dealers, four of whom lived in Lavenham. There were three pig dealers
and one cattle dealer and it is certain they would form a link between
the farmer and the butcher.

Trades and services

Lavenham was undoubtedly an independent village for it had developed a closely integrated economy. There were forty shops at the turn
of the century, but in addition there were people like plumbers, brick-
makers and many associated with the building industry who found
work within the village. A doctor was also on hand, living in the large
house in Lady Street known as Grove House. He was a qualified sur-
geon as well as physician and no doubt a very busy man. He was also
the agent for the Suffolk Alliance Insurance Society. No doubt some
of his income would be derived from patients who were covered by
the company in case of illness, for at this time medical attention had
to be funded by the patient.

The law of demand and supply operated freely then in Lavenham. If
there was a need someone sought to supply it, as they did in many
isolated communities. In these days of quick and almost universal
transport a different picture prevails, with centralization of services

*Baker's
deliveries*

Mr and Mrs Rampling outside their shoemaker's shop in Barn Street

and supplies – a matter for regret, for there is no real substitute for the village shop with its good, efficient and above all friendly service.

The boot and shoe maker and repairer illustrates the point. He was a most important person in the community. In the age of the motor car we cannot appreciate the amount of walking undertaken by many people a hundred years ago. The farmworker is a classic case, for he would leave his cottage in the village early in the morning and go on foot to his place of work, in many cases more than a mile. If he worked with horses he would walk constantly all day and much of the time on rough ground. At night he would return on foot to his cottage. He would walk more miles in a day than many of us today walk in a month.

A team of two horses would plough one acre of land in a working day and the horseman (and the horses) would cover a distance of at least eight miles in a day. On jobs where the horses might travel faster, it might have been more. In such circumstances boots would wear quickly. It is no wonder that there was enough work to keep seven boot and shoe makers and repairers busy. Today our chief concern is how our footwear looks. We have to be in 'the fashion'. The question is no longer 'How long will it wear?'

In 1880 there were thirteen dressmakers in the village. In an age of mass-produced clothes (the Marks and Spencer era) we cannot readily appreciate a time when so many women were needed to produce clothing, and for everyone, not just for the well-off. Many garments would have been made of the type of woollen cloth known as serge which used to be woven in Lavenham. Women needed hard-wearing skirts particularly if they were going out to work in factories, or in the fields. As old photographs show, the cloth was very drab and utilitarian, except for 'Sunday best' and special occasions when something a little brighter and more decorative would be worn. People on low incomes (the majority) could ill-afford to buy anything that was not hard-wearing since it was likely that in due course it would be taken for everyday wear.

The chemist's shop was very different from the place it is today. Half the shop was devoted to animal medicines and remedies, alongside which were other requirements for the farm such as feeding stuffs for calves, salt licks and disinfectant, Stockholm tar for dressing the infected feet of sheep and cattle, and dipping powders for sheep. There was a link between the chemist and the vet just as there is today between the doctor and the pharmacist.

There was one hairdresser in the Market Square next to the Angel, who appeared to employ one man. They must have been kept very busy considering the size of the population, but this was also an age when there were many 'amateur' hairdressers (or barbers) about. Men who had full-time jobs would often develop sufficient skills with hand clippers and scissors to make a reasonable job of cutting the hair of their friends – a source of a little extra income.

Much trade with the farming community was done by the ironmonger, Mr A Lee of the High Street. He was also a bell hanger and gas fitter. An account to George Mumford of Hill Farm dated 1891 includes: '1 Horn Lantern, 3 Levers, Water Pot and new Bottle 2 doz. Ploughshares, 1 Packet of candles, 1 Tin of knife polish, 2 Pails and a hard brush'. No retailer carried such a variety of merchandise as the ironmonger. His shop must have been like an Aladdin's Cave, as are some still left in rural areas today.

Thomas Baker's windmill on the Bury Road

These well-documented facts demonstrate how closely knit the village was and how dependent the inhabitants were upon one another. No doubt such closeness would give rise to difficulties at times for in a small community everyone knows everyone else. A grievance or a problem would soon become common currency and might easily sour relationships.

In addition to the craftsmen and tradesmen already mentioned, the following were to be found living in the village: three hay trussers, three pig dealers, one cattle dealer, one horse dealer, two woodmen, two barn shovel makers and two hurdle makers, all very closely involved with farming.

Farming-related industries

One of the most important industries subsidiary to farming was the corn mill in Prentice Street established in 1865 by Thomas Baker. Prior to this he had developed a maltings at the top of Lady Street and had used a windmill for grinding corn, the remains of which still stands on the hill overlooking Lavenham on the Bury Road.

Much traffic passed between the farms and these three sites: corn to

34

be ground into flour or cattle feed and barley for malting. The change from the wind-powered mill to the steam-driven mill in the village provided additional employment, and the trade further expanded with the development of the railway. There were close links between the Baker Mill and the farms, and beyond to the farms in neighbouring parishes. The mill remains in Prentice Street, converted into dwellings.

Three years on from the opening of the Baker Mill, Lavenham was chosen as the first centre in England for the production of sugar from beet. The instigator of this enterprise appeared to have had no connection with farming. He was a successful merchant, James Duncan of Mincing Lane, London. In 1868 he opened a substantial factory to extract sugar from beet on the Lower Road near to the railway station. He was clearly a man of some vision who was willing to take considerable risk with his capital. The factory was sited on the bank of the river Brad, no doubt in order to ensure a good supply of water for cleaning the beet prior to processing, and a railway siding was laid into the site.

Local farmers showed great enthusiasm for the project and adapted quickly to this new challenge. The *Suffolk and Essex Free Press* reports a meeting of the Lavenham Farmer's Club on 1st April 1869 at the Swan Inn, Lavenham.* A paper entitled 'The Growth of Beet

*A transcription of the report is in Lavenham Guildhall Museum.

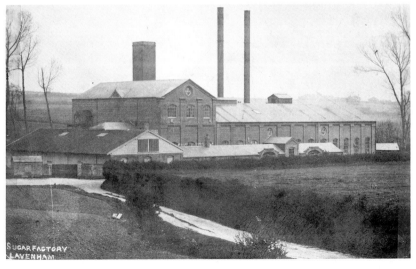

The sugar factory in Lower Road

Root for Sugar' was delivered by Mr R. Hawkins, a highly respected farmer whose land was just over the parish boundary at Milden. Mr Hawkins described his own method of growing beet. The first essential, he maintained, was good ploughing. The land should be given a good dressing of farmyard manure and of guano (dried seabird droppings imported from South America). He contended that his methods had proved their worth by producing successful crops of beet. He believed that the development of the beet factory was most beneficial to the area, and all would be well if markets could be found for the sugar produced, at a remunerative price.

Alas, this was not to be. Beet sugar was in competition with imported cane sugar and could not be produced at a competitive price. Mr Duncan played his part, the farmers worked hard to produce beet for processing but in the end production had to stop as buyers could not be found at the price needed for economic production. The business had struggled for three years and was closed in 1871. It was re-opened in 1885 but again as a result of cheap imports it was closed within a short time.

Mr Duncan's experiment was later vindicated when in the late 1930s the Government lent its support to the growing of sugar beet on a large scale throughout the United Kingdom, and a large grid of factories was built across the country. Unfortunately for Lavenham the factory had burned down in 1905, and several years later it was demolished. For a brief time before its demolition it had been occupied by the leading milk producer of the area, Tom Norman, who bred some very high yielding Friesian cows and developed a national reputation in milk production records.

Mention has been made of the factories developed for the production of horsehair fabric and coconut matting, which provided work for families of farmworkers when incomes were low. In due course the factories had to close as markets for the products began to shrink. Lavenham did not escape a period of depression and many members of the community experienced great hardship. Mechanization in agriculture was being introduced and as this gathered pace the labour force was being reduced. These were uncertain and worrying times for the people of Lavenham. Many people left the village in search of employment and the population fell from 1,800 to 1,500. The feeling of independence and interdependence was fast disappearing.

4 The horse in the life of Lavenham

Apart from the occasional sight of a horse being ridden through the village on hire from the local riding stables, or a hunter or two grazing in the paddock near the farms, horses tend to be forgotten now in Lavenham. This was not the case in 1880 and for many years after.

One of the commonest sounds to be heard in the streets was that of the steady plod of horses' hooves, the jingle of harness and the rattle of iron-clad wheels from cart and waggon. At almost any time of the day they could be seen leaving the farmyards to take up work in nearby fields, and moving from field to field as the work demanded. Horses and waggons would leave the farms with loads of corn on their way to Baker's Mill in Prentice Street and return loaded with milled corn for cattle, pigs, sheep and horses on the farms.

From time to time, unburdened by cart or harness, they would be taken to one of the blacksmiths in the village to be fitted with a new set of shoes. They could be seen at the station picking up loads of seed corn from Ipswich or brewer's grain from the Greene King Brewery at Bury St Edmunds.

Some of the traders in Lavenham owned horse drawn-vehicles for use in delivering to places outside the village, and in addition there were two registered carriers making regular journeys to nearby towns. Their schedule is recorded:

To Bury   Wednesday and Saturday: Mr Keeble
To Ipswich   Monday and Thursday: Mr Mann
To Melford   Wedneday: Mr Mann
To Sudbury   Monday, Tuesday, Wednesday and Friday: Mr Keeble

Fifty years earlier a coach left the Black Lion Hotel in the High Street every Thursday for London, and although in 1880 Lavenham did have a coachman, William Walker of Church Street, he would have been undertaking local journeys. The London coach would have ceased to run when the railway reached Lavenham in 1865, and prob-

Mr Rudd driving a wedding carriage

ably before. Lavenham also had its own livery company and one of the best known names in this field was Mr Rudd, who set up his business some years later in premises in Water Street which are now part of the Swan Hotel.

To add to these, many licences were issued to businessmen and farmers who wished to have their own transport in the form of a horse and carriage. These licences were issued by an officer of the Inland Revenue who lived at what is known today as the Great House Restaurant in the Market Place. The officer in 1881 was a William Harrison. The house must have been the Inland Revenue office, for when he later he moved on the new officer also lived there. The licence cost 15 shillings – quite expensive.

A large population
No records exist of the number of horses, but as Lavenham had its own mill and maltings, its own railway station, and a number of traders using their own transport, in addition to the numbers used on farms, the horse population must have been very large. Within the

parish boundary some 3,000 acres were under cultivation, and in any work undertaken on the farms the horse would be involved. Ploughing, cultivating, drilling, harvesting and carting made constant demands on the availability of horses. Family members today whose forbears were involved confirm that up to 20 horses were being used for work at Lavenham Hall around 1900, and as they were bred on the farm, there could have been another 10 being prepared for work or for sale.

There were rough and ready measurements of the rates of work accomplished by horses in a day of eight hours. These were affected by the job being done and the type of soil being worked. A clay soil would need more horses than would be required on a sandy soil for the same job, and in any case progress would always be slower on heavy soil. The weather would also play its part, for if the soil was wet and sticky this was an additional handicap. Despite these variations some measures were accepted and used by farmers in planning their work. In this part of Suffolk, these were:

Ploughing	1 acre per 8-hour day, 2 horses
Drilling	10 acres per 8-hour day, 2 horses
Harrowing	20 acres per 8-hour day, 2 horses
Rolling	10 acres per 8-hour day, 1 horse

It follows that on a farm of 200 acres where most of it was under the plough, two horses would be needed for 200 days to complete the ploughing each year. As the time for ploughing – dictated by the season and the weather – was limited, not more than about 100 days, a minimum of four horses were required for this one basic operation. In addition other jobs would be going on at the same time requiring maybe another four horses. In other words eight to ten horses would be needed on 200 acres.

Thus some 200 horses must have been kept on Lavenham farms at this time, for amongst this number would be young horses being prepared for work or sale, and some brood mares taken out of the work force as they got nearer to foaling. A further 50 would be working about the village transporting a whole range of materials, including coal, corn, milk, goods to and from the station and the nearby towns of Sudbury, Bury, Long Melford and Ipswich.

Two other factors add weight to these estimates. There were six qualified blacksmiths living in the parish, and in 1900 three forges were operating for a brief period. There were also four qualified saddlers and harness makers at work, and two wheelwrights' premises in use around this time.

Breeds and breeding

The dominant breed of working horse was the Suffolk Punch, with slightly shorter legs, strong neck and shoulders and deep barrel compared with other breeds. The Suffolk Punch was thought by many to be the finest breed in the British Isles, but some would claim that this accolade should rightly go to the Shire or Clydesdale. It would not be wise to press such claims if you are within the Suffolk county boundary, even today.

Some very fine horses, including prize winners at national shows, were bred at the Lavenham Hall stud. At Lavenham Hill Farm the Percheron (a breed which originated in France) held sway, and several fine horses were bred there at this time.

Lavenham became famous for its Horse Fair. This gave an opportunity for farmers and breeders to sell any surplus horses they had each year. It was held on Monday and the next day, Shrove Tuesday, and is thought to have been linked to the Feast of St Blaise, the patron saint of woolcombers (celebrated originally on 3rd February).

The fair was a time when the village was packed with visitors, some coming for a day out and to meet friends and relatives and some to do business. The most important buyers would come from London, looking for suitable horses for work on London streets. The hotels would be full to overflowing as would the public houses. The men from London would stay overnight at one or other of the residential hotels.

Sir Alfred Munnings, the famous horse painter, frequently visited the fair, no doubt in search of material for his work. The atmosphere of the day is captured admirably in his own account of the fair of 1898:

Lavenham Horse Fair? what a sight. This famous fair of heavy draught Horses eclipsed anything of its kind I had ever seen. "The Swan" was then unaltered and not the swell place it is today. I got a room there in spite of it being packed with a breed of men long since gone. Men with fat jowls, wearing wide brimmed bowlers or half-high hats, who came from London to buy heavy horses for London work – for railway companies vans, brewers drays and hosts of other trades. We went from Inn yard to Inn yard where straw

At Lavenham Horse Fair, near the Swan Hotel. The man in the half-tall hat was a Mr Pattle, who seems to answer to Munnings' description of a well-fed purple faced man. Those watching appear to stand in a certain amount of awe of him.

lay strewn on the ground, and those well-fed, clean shaven, purple faced men were already seeing horses trotted up and down in the yards, in the main street, and on the Green up near the Church with its tall tower. (Sir Alfred Munnings, *An Artist's Life*, 1950)

This must be one of the last eye-witness descriptions of the fair, which not long afterwards ceased to be held.

The horseman

Many of the men living in and around Lavenham would have daily contact with the horse; working with them in the fields carrying out the whole range of operations such as ploughing, preparing the land for sowing, sowing, rolling (a job for the apprentice horseman) and hoeing to keep the crops free of weeds. Then, as the weeks passed, the crops would ripen and harvest would commence, with cutting and binding the sheaves, (a process which had been mechanized some ten year earlier). The final act would be to carry the sheaves on loaded waggons for stacking in the 'rick yard' near the farm.

Riding home at day's end. The horse would know the way.

This was a time when men and horses were fully stretched, working until dark to beat the weather. Sheaves which stood in the field beyond their allotted time and got wet made life difficult for they had to be fully dry before being stacked. Despite the problems the harvest was a pleasant time for it was the culmination of a year of hard work for men and horses.

The head horseman, in charge of a stable of eight or ten horses, would be required to live out of Lavenham in one of the cottages near the farm buildings, for the horses needed frequent attention. In the winter an early morning feed before the day's work and one in the evening was necessary for horses working as hard as these were. In addition to the head man, a number of the other workers on the farm would also work the horses, but many of these did live in Lavenham.

It is difficult today to fully appreciate the bond which existed between the man and his horses (certain horses would be allocated to each man for long periods) and not easy to understand the level of skill required from both. We pride ourselves on our skill in driving a car, but compared to working a horse and plough it is child's play. And for much of the time the man was working two horses together. The horse is an intelligent animal, and very strong. He or she is a creature of habit and can be trained to do certain things, but he relies on his master for guidance. He can be co-operative and he can be stubborn. Understanding the horse's character is part of the skill of getting the best out of him. Each was an individual and had a name to which he would respond. A man who never talked to his horse would fail to master the craft of horsemanship, and would not be allowed to work with them if it could be avoided.

Horses in village life

Horses featured prominently in the life of the village. Children would stand in the streets to see them pass, the bolder ones hoping they might get a ride on the waggon, whilst the old men would cast a critical eye on the horses, no doubt passing comment on how fit or unfit they looked – never so good as they used to look in the 'old days'.

There would also be constant movement of materials about the village, as the horsehair and raw materials for coconut matting came into the village by road or rail, and the finished product went out. The 'light' carriers would be off to Sudbury or Bury and then returning. The coalman too would be a familiar sight on his weekly round delivering his sacks up and down the streets, for although wood played a large part in warming the larger houses, coal was widely used in the smaller houses and cottages. Another common sight would have been the milkman on his daily round in pony and cart with churns and cans. The man delivering oil for lamps and stoves would be seen from time to time in the out-lying areas, for although gas was made in Lavenham from 1862 onwards, pipes did not reach all areas round the village.

In many respects then, the horse played a dominant role in the economy both on the farms and in the village itself, and it was only slowly that it gave way to the influence of the internal combustion engine in the form of buses, lorries, cars and tractors. For a period, steam was harnessed to some aspects of the farm and the factory but this is a story in itself. Probably the largest influence steam had on Lavenham was the coming of the railway.

5 The farm worker, key man of the village

Both in terms of numbers and in his contribution to the economy, the farmworker dominated the village. It would have been impossible to walk the streets or enter a pub in Lavenham in 1880 without coming across a group of them. It is almost certain that they would be discussing some aspect of their work, possibly making reference to the weather, since the changing weather patterns had a far-reaching effect on what they did and when they did it.

As mentioned earlier, John Woodgate Baker, who farmed a fair proportion of the land in Lavenham in the early nineteen hundreds, kept a diary of his farming activities at Brights and Netherhall farms. At first his entries were short and to the point but as time passed they became much more detailed. It is clear that the weather was much on his mind.

1908
Michaelmas – A splendid Autumn, all work done in excellent order to Christmas.

1909
Dry february. Commenced sowing Peas and Beans March very wintery, frost from beginning to finish
Beautiful April and May weather rectifying previous months. June wet throughout and big flood 25th and 26th — thunderstorms
July wet throughout
About 15 fine dry very hot days the early part of August, the remainder continuously wet and cold.
September all wet weather. October all wet weather – a very great proportion of corn carted in bad conditions.
Commenced harvest Aug.13th left off in October. October 29th and 30th big floods
Oct. 25th and 26th drilled Autumn Barley – Netherhall and twelve acres Rivets at Brights.
A wet November – roots came badly. December very wet 4" of rain measured – had several floods. A most disagreeable year. Thatched Wheat stack Sept.1st
(John Woodgate Baker, diaries, Lavenham Guildhall Museum)

Mr Baker was more than glad to see the end of 1909. Harvest had started full of promise, but as early as September he needed to thatch his first rick as a result of continuous rain, and of course the labour was available as most other operations were at a standstill. In a normal time thatching of ricks would be done when some of the harvest was in, and the pressures were off.

These diary entries demonstrate the major part played by the weather in the daily lives of the farming community. Bad weather disturbed all the farmer's well-laid plans, and for the worker it often meant that his job became more difficult because of adverse soil conditions. It also meant that he had to work harder to try to make up for lost time. The diary entries show that the resultant crops were often badly affected in terms of yield and quality. Bad weather from a farming point of view can also mean that conditions become too dry. The ground becomes hard and cannot be worked or, which is worse, seeds fail to germinate and crops stop growing. In these conditions livestock also suffer for lack of grazing. It is no wonder that throughout the ages weather has dominated the farming community.

A skilled man

Many attempts have been made to portray the life and character of the farmworker of the 19th and early 20th century, and some of these are highly descriptive of his life. Some see him as a plodding individual, somewhat limited in outlook, subservient to his master, others see him as a stubborn individual unprepared to change his ways come what may. Most descriptions fall short of reality and many lack understanding of the real essence of the life he led. The cardinal error arises from the misguided belief that the farmworker was an unskilled labourer – as his title of 'farm labourer' implies. The word itself, with its meaning of 'one who labours', over time came to mean 'one of limited skills'. Such a description could not have been true of the farmworkers of Lavenham or of anywhere else, for there was no task on any farm which did not call for a degree of skill and knowledge, and many tasks required a high level of both.

Although the farmer as manager of land and men had his own knowledge and skill which enabled him to make a success of his enterprise, there was a large measure of delegation required. His success was inextricably bound up with the skill of his men.

Ploughing at Hall Farm in the early 1900s

The previous chapter looked at the importance of the horse in farming and how the power he possessed had to be channelled into the various operations by the men who were in charge of him. The skill required by such men is well illustrated in one of the most important basic tasks, that of ploughing the land.

The man would arrive early at the stable, and his first job was to carry water to the stable or draw it from the tap in the stable. The horses would be offered as much water as they would take. (They had a long day ahead and would loose much fluid as a result of sweating). The man would then give them a feed in the manger – a mixture of oats and chaff. As they fed he would groom and brush them – all part of the preparation for the day. Grooming was not done simply to make a horse look good, it had a stimulating effect on the animal. The man's experience would tell him something about the mood of the horse – for they are subject to change just as humans are. The horse might not be feeling too well and might refuse his food. If that happened the horseman would turn to a colleague for a second opinion. Some medication might be required or in an extreme case a vet would be called.

Remedies for ailments in farm animals were limited at this time, just as they were for people – but diagnosis was well advanced. Nursing played a major part in the restoration of animals back to fitness, using what came to be known in later years as 'old fashioned remedies'. A good horseman would have a range of such remedies at his disposal. A number of these are contained in the notebook of a horseman who worked in Lavenham, and the following is an example.

To cure a horse of a bad cold. Take 2 eggs put in half pint of vinegar bind them down from the air 48 hrs. Take and beat them well with same vinegar with two tablespoonsful of honey and mix them together give that to a horse each morning an hour after give him a bran mash and a half pint of linseed boil them in 2 pints of water mix them well together put in the manger boiling hot. After this mixture take a handful of horehound ditto rue ditto featherfew ditto mullen leaf ditto marsh mallows ditto elder leaves ditto agrimony ditto balm then boil this in a gallon of water till it wasted to three pints in this 2 eggs to a pint and a half. 2 tablespoonsful of honey give him a pint and a half after an hour.

Another example:

For a horse that is Feeble in Stomach. Give him a quarter of an ounce of gentian powder in a bran mash three times a week after water.

(Horseman's notebook, Lavenham Guildhall Museum)

The first example is a remarkable concoction and would almost baffle a qualified dispenser. These men had an extensive knowledge of herbs. Sick animals will seek out such herbs in the hedgerows even today, which suggests that many of the recorded remedies were based on scientific information and observation.

If the horses were fit, the horseman would then harness them up using harness hanging behind the horse in the stable – each horse had its own 'tack'. The choice of harness would depend on the job to be done, and if they were going off to plough they would fit a back band instead of the saddle, used when horses were being worked with waggons or carts.

Thus equipped, the horseman would move off to the field where the single furrow plough would be waiting on the headland. If several horses were going out of the stable in the morning there was a hierarchy of departure which was sacrosanct. The head horseman would go first, followed in order by the second horseman and so on. Where possible the same order would operate in the evening, the head man again leading.

The ploughman would normally take two horses to the job and on arrival at the field he would back them up to the front of the plough for hitching up. This was simple for experienced horses, but should he have a young horse even this task might prove difficult – generally speaking horses do not like to move backwards. The team, as they then became, were now ready for work and the first task was to mark a 'headland' all round the field. This provided a space round the edge of the land to be left unploughed until all the middle of the field was completed. He would then mark out the field in 'bouts' or 'lands'. In effect he ploughed ridges at intervals across the field. In most cases these were known as 'split ridges', which meant that a furrow could be ploughed outwards. The team would turn and come down the other side again and this furrow would also be ploughed outwards. He would then turn into this furrow and plough it back into the centre. The plough would actually lift the existing furrow back into its original position. He would do the same with the original furrow. Thus all the land was actually turned over.

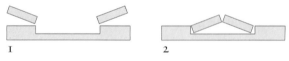

I   2

Splitting the ridge

This was a highly skilled piece of work for a first straight furrow meant straight furrows throughout (with experience it was possible to correct this but again it called for great skill). It has to be remembered that the horseman was doing several things at once: driving the horse by means of a plough line held in the hands, by which he exercised control and kept the horse going in an absolutely straight line; holding and guiding the plough to mark a straight line; and controlling the depth of the plough by the angle at which it was held – a gigantic task (driving a tractor and plough is simple by comparison). If the field was not flat there was a further challenge.

The majority of farmworkers worked with horses, carrying out jobs such as harrowing, rolling and horsehoeing, and these, although not as demanding as ploughing, needed skills of which we know little today.

When mechanical drills were introduced they were designed to deliver certain rates of seed and had to be adjusted to suit the particular seed being drilled. This called for mathematical ability, otherwise the seed would run out before the field was complete or, at the other end of the scale, seed which should have been in the ground would be in the sack. The result in either case would be a minor financial disaster, for the crop would fall far short of expectations. Even before the advent of the drill, when the fiddle was being used, the same calculations were required.

Stamina and strength were also demanded. The horseman would be walking up to ten miles a day for six days a week in all kinds of weather, be it hot or freezing cold. Often he would be expected to carry on in the rain, at least until the ground got too sticky. Richard Jefferies, in his portrait of the Wiltshire farm worker,* talks of him being slow and ponderous in his gait. Is there any wonder? Most of us today would be prostrate after a few hours of such exacting work let alone ponderous and slow.

Some farmworkers were not involved in horsework, but their skills

*In a letter to *The Times*, November 1872.

Drilling at Hall Farm in the early 1900s

Shearing sheep on a Lavenham farm

lay in other directions. Hedging, ditching and draining were common tasks and they involved different abilities and knowledge; they, too, required strength and stamina. They involved the use of hand tools such as scythes, fagging hooks, slashers, bill hooks and a range of draining tools.

The first drains were formed by digging out a trench, starting at the lowest point where water would run into a ditch and working back to the central area of the field and in a number of other ways. The bottom of the trench would be filled with hedge trimmings and then all the soil returned to the trench. Later earthenware pipes were used in place of hedge trimmings to convey water to the ditches.

Digging trenches was an exacting operation for they had to remain stable over a period of time until pipes were laid. An unskilled worker would find that as he dug, the sides of the trench would break and fill the bottom, all of which would have to be taken out before the pipes were laid. Above all there would have to be a small gradient in the trench so that water would run away and not lodge at any point along its length. The drainer would have to understand soil types and levels and be able to use all the hand tools with precision. He also needed stamina, in conditions which were often wet and sticky.

Farmworkers concerned with the care and management of livestock needed particular perception and knowledge. Animals will only grow and thrive in the correct environment, and to a large extent the stockman is responsible for this, within the limits of the buildings at his disposal. Stock require the right temperature and atmosphere, regular and adequate feeding and early attention when disorders strike. Where a number of animals are housed together this can be critical as diseases spread rapidly. Young animals in particular when they are weaned from their dams need special care and observation. Calves and young pigs were very vulnerable as were new born lambs. Sheep were very much a specialists job and shepherds have always commanded considerable respect from the non-farming communities. The same would have been true of the cattleman and the pigman.

All this is true today but was even more so a hundred years ago when housing standards for livestock were often far from ideal. Perhaps the job then called for an even higher level of skill from the stockman than it does today.

The work of the stockman

A century ago the livestock population in Lavenham was quite high, although the agricultural scene was dominated by arable crops. Sheep were present in fairly large numbers, and pigs were to be found on most farms. A few milking cows were kept but the largest sector was fattening cattle imported into Suffolk from Ireland, Scotland and the north, and some were bred on farms around Lavenham. The cattle would be brought to Bury St Edmunds market where they would be auctioned and sold to local buyers. The movement of livestock was made easier when the railway was opened between Bury St Edmunds and Lavenham. One or two people today can still remember seeing cattle being driven through the village from the station to the farms.

The cattle were kept in covered yards through the winter and fed on turnips, mangolds and straw, with some oats. Some hay was used but only in the latter stages of the fattening process. When the grass started to grow in the spring these cattle would be turned out on to the permanent pastures to be 'finished off' (fattened) ready for the livestock market. In Mr Baker's diary there are frequent references to this system of managing fattening cattle.

Nov. 9th 1903	Put in yard 10 bullocks
June 15th 1915	Beef making 14/- per stone [70p]
Oct 30th 1918	Bought 20 bullocks ex Bury Market average £16-17s
March 1916	3 Beeflings made £24-15s at 13 months old £19-10s for a year old and for a red poll (14 months) £21-10s

Beef at 70p per stone is the equivalent of 5p per lb. Today finished cattle in the same market would sell at 60p per lb.

Although fattening beef was sometimes profitable the main purpose of the system was the production of farmyard manure. Straw was littered in the yards each day and trodden in by the cattle, the straw and dung serving to produce the manure for spreading on the land, thus returning some of the nutrients taken out by the crops, and also supplying the essential humus for a healthy soil. This practice was widespread throughout the arable crop growing areas in the United Kingdom a hundred years ago and it would still be claimed today that this was the soundest system of crop growing ever developed, when coupled with a proper crop rotation programme.

The key person in the system was the stockman or cattleman. On the larger farms, caring for the livestock would have been his main task, as it was at Hall Farm and Park Farm where relatively large numbers of livestock were kept. On the smaller farms the person involved would have been drafted in from the general staff, but he would develop his skills and gain experience under the watchful eye of the farmer.

In all cases his perception, his attention to detail and an understanding of animal behaviour were all required to make a success of the tasks of rearing cattle to the point ready for sale. He needed to be able to judge the appetites of those in his care – and this would change as they grew. No two animals are alike and he would need to be able to identify them as he watched their development from day to day. He would be able to spot the 'boss' animals and the underlings and deal with them accordingly.

His routines of feeding would have to be regular and well spread out, aiming at keeping the cattle content. Only so would they grow and put on weight. Hungry cattle become restless and do not gain weight. In freezing weather he would need to see that water was available and that as much shelter as possible was provided to protect the cattle from winds and draughts. He would be looking for 'bloom' on the coats of his animals and watching to see that they were licking themselves regularly – all signs that the cattle were thriving. He would have to be alert to the beast which had isolated itself from the others and had lost its appetite – a sure sign of the onset of some disorder. Such a beast would have to be housed separately for special care and also to check the spread of infection.

If he were head stockman he would also be responsible for the pigs on the farm. His chief task would be to ensure that the sows maintained a regular breeding pattern, that they were given proper attention during farrowing and that young pigs grew rapidly before they were weaned. The feeding and care would have to be carried out to a high standard.

The biggest demand of all was on his skills of observation. Every animal, large or small, needed to be seen each day. If something was wrong and went unobserved the animal could deteriorate rapidly and perhaps die because it was too late to bring it back to health. The death of an animal in a small bunch could mean the difference between the profit or loss of the bunch.

When we look at the range of jobs undertaken by the farmworker, he no longer appears to be the slow witted, plodding, dour individual portrayed by some misguided writers. The list is endless: it includes caring for and working with horses, feeding and looking after livestock, shepherding, hedge trimming and hedge laying (a very highly skilled craft), ditching, draining and fencing.

As well as being able to use a range of hand tools, including scythes and axes, the farmworker was expected to operate and keep in good running order a range of machines, such as seed drills, corn binders and grass mowers. Many would be able to build corn ricks and thatch them, build a hay rick (a particularly difficult job), and load a waggon securely with sheaves of corn or hay so that the load would be transported safely over the rough track to the farmyard. Many of the tools the farmworker used had to be sharpened regularly, so he would generally have his own set. Tools were not always provided by the employer.

Many men could do a large number of these jobs, whereas others

Large families lived in small cottages (Pump Court, front and rear, since demolished).

might specialize, but of none could it be said that no skill was required, and I would argue strongly that the title of labourer was a travesty of the true worth of a man.

Hard conditions at home

In Lavenham parish in 1881 there were 22 farmers and 206 farm-workers. A few lived in cottages on the farms but the majority were to be found living in cottages in the village. Some of the cottages were owned by employers and some by private landlords; very few were owned by farmworkers, unless they had been passed down through the family. In some cases the farmer would charge no rent for his cottage, but that meant that if for some reason the man lost his job, possibly as a result of illness, or because he did not please the farmer, he would lose his house when the job was terminated. If this happened the man and his family would face real hardship.

Of the 206 farmworkers, 127 were married and 79 were single. 74 of the single men still lived with their parents, who were generally also farmworkers. An additional 59 children (mostly daughters) of farmworkers were employed in horsehair weaving, and seven young men were employed in the production of coconut matting. The total number of children at school or at work, born to married farmworkers, was 418. This meant that the average size of a farmworker's family in Lavenham was four children. In all, some 650 people were dependent on farming for a living.

It is clear that the farmworker and his family lived in extremely overcrowded conditions. Many of the cottages were very small and in some cases consisted of one room downstairs and only one bedroom. The 1881 census record shows that in some cases married children were living in their parents' home. There was one family of 11 children, one with nine, and several with six. Many households contained a mother, father and their children and in addition the married son or daughter would be living with them. In one or two cases a grandchild was also recorded as being in residence. This must have been an intolerable situation but one to which there was no alternative, until some other accommodation could be found at a price the young couple could afford. It is doubtful if any cottage or house in Lavenham was big enough to accommodate some of the larger families.

The sanitary arrangements existing in the village in 1880 and for many years after were quite inadequate for such conditions of overcrowding. Water supplies to houses were variable both in quality and quantity. Much of it had to be obtained from wells in the gardens or in some cases from a communal supply. Many of the cottages were dilapidated, cold and draughty with a fire of wood or coal in one room only.

Up to 1862 lighting was by candle and oil lamp until the gasworks were opened. The introduction of gas into houses after this would depend on whether its installation could be afforded, or, more importantly, whether the householder could afford to pay for the supply. Winter evenings in conditions described above must have been grim, with large families huddling over meagre fires. Not the cosy scene that we sometimes imagine might have been the case. Cooking facilities were primitive, either on an open fire or by the means of an oven that rarely kept hot enough to make a successful meal; and washday in the depths of winter must have been a considerable challenge to the housewife.

Diseases such as tuberculosis, scarlet fever and diphtheria were rife in the village, mainly as a result of overcrowded and insanitary conditions but also due to malnutrition. In short, life in 1880 for the farmworker and his family was a continuous struggle against enormous odds.

Necessities and luxuries

It is no coincidence that there were nine public houses in the village. Some relief from the depressed conditions had to be sought and the pubs were the only places where this could be found. The Church had a part to play but on a different level. Unfortunately in some cases money, which should have been used to care for the family, found its way to the pub, for human nature changes little even in our more affluent times. The man and his wife would, at times, gather in the pub where they would be sure of meeting their circle of friends, many of them being their workmates. Here they could speak their mind and indulge in a measure of enjoyment, exchanging tales of the day and recounting the incidents of the week. Many of them would have their favourite local, the choice being made on the basis of the particular beer on sale.

In summer the pubs would often be dominated by the farmworkers, for hay and corn harvest were thirsty times. Much beer was consumed during the day and sometimes in the evenings. It was traditional for a certain amount of beer to be available to the farmworkers at harvest time, supplied by the farmer. It used to be said that this beer would not be as strong as that sold in pubs, on the grounds that a drunken worker would not be much use in the harvest field. At threshing time the farmer always supplied 'drinkings', usually beer, and also bread and cheese. The reason for this was that the threshing tackle was on hire and the farmer wanted to keep it running for as long as possible during daylight hours. He supplied food in order that stoppages for eating were kept as short as possible.

Some slight alleviation of the harsh conditions suffered by farmworkers and their families came from the fact that most of the cottages had a piece of land attached, which varied in size, but in many cases was large enough to enable them to supplement their food supplies by growing vegetables and potatoes. Some had facilities for keeping a pig and possibly some poultry to supply eggs. A pig was luxury indeed, particularly when it was finally slaughtered. The parts of the pig which could not be kept beyond a few days would be distributed amongst neighbours. Much of this was regarded as a delicacy although today it would be designated as offal. Much brawn was also made and distributed amongst friends and relations.

In Lavenham in 1880 another factor contributed towards the reduc-

Workers outside the horsehair weaving factory in Barn Street, wearing their 'Sunday best'

tion of hardship, which was not available in most country areas. Coconut matting and horsehair was being manufactured on a factory basis. Forty girls (daughters of farmworkers) worked in the horsehair weaving factories and several young men (sons of farmworkers) found employment in the matting factory. Welcome as these jobs were, their impact on most families was marginal, for the average wage of a farmworker in Lavenham at this time was only 15 shillings (75p) a week. Farmworkers were paid much less than other craftsmen.

Food prices at the time were as follows:

Eggs: 10d per dozen (4¹/₂p)
Milk: 4d per quart (1¹/₂p)
Beef: 9d per pound (3³/₄p)
Pork: 8d per pound (3¹/₂p)
Lamb: 12d per pound (5p)

57

Beans: 2d per pound (½p)
Cabbage: 1d per pound (½p)
Potatoes: ½d per pound (⅛p)
Butter: 12d per pound (5p)
Margarine: 6d per pound (2½p)
Cheese: 10d per pound (4½p)

For a family of four the basic requirements for food per week would be: 3lb of beef, 2lb of pork, 2lb of beans, 4lb of cabbage, 20lb of potatoes, 1½lb of margarine, 4lb of cheese, 7 quarts of milk, 2 dozen eggs, 10lb of flour, and sugar, lard etc. Assuming all the items were purchased, a total sum of 60p would be required. This leaves an amount of 15p to meet all other living expenses, including oil, candles and possibly coal. There would be little left over for beer.

Such figures reveal the reality of the struggle for survival of the agricultural workers in Lavenham in 1880. There were some improvements during the years ahead but they were not sustained. The position was the result of an economic system which produced extremes of poverty and wealth. The food producers were the most important section of society and yet they went unrecognized for their undoubted skill and were inadequately rewarded for the vital role they played in the economy.

6 The traditional husbandry of Lavenham

As the 20 century moves towards its end there is concern in all quarters at the state of farming in Britain. Farmers themselves are facing a financial crisis which they say is the worst since the 1930s. They say this has been brought about by the government's mishandling of the situation and in particular by the European Common Agricultural Policy.

How present-day farming methods came about

Agriculture in the United Kingdom since the 1947 Agriculture Act has been supported by the Treasury. Initially it was necessary in order to meet the nation's need for food. After the Second World War there were international shortages of food and the pressure was on to produce as much as possible from our own resources and to rely less on imported food. Government policy was therefore directed to self-sufficiency. A free advisory service was developed from the ideas adopted during the war when farmers were directed as to what crops they should grow and and to some extent how they should grow them. The same applied to livestock production.

The '47 Act, as it came to be known, was two pronged. One was to provide incentives by way of subsidies and the other was to make advice freely available. This took the form of a field service of well-qualified personnel who were trained to advise on all technical aspects of the industry. Another of their duties was to make the industry aware of new systems and techniques, and ways and means of improving efficiency. The drive was on to produce more and more food and to produce it as cheaply as possible. Subsidies to the industry took many forms, from acreage payments for the ploughing up of old pasture land, to a cash payment for the application of lime (where necessary) and special tax allowances on the purchase of farm machinery. Payments were made on an acreage basis to encourage farmers to grow potatoes, sugar beet and other selected crops.

Farmers were also supported in the market-place by the government setting a guaranteed price for various crops and livestock. Before the commencement of each farming year the Minister of Agriculture and his officials would sit down with the farmers' leaders and agree a range of prices which would prevail for the twelve months ahead. It was generally a very hard bargaining exercise on both sides – the government constrained by the conflicting demands of different crops and services, and the Farmers' Unions wanting to secure the best deal for all its members, large and small. The central issue was the question of the country's food supplies. As time went on and food became more plentiful the system changed and grants and subsidies were gradually reduced. Advice was still available on a wide front and was always free until recent years when some charges were made for certain services.

Another aspect of the help to the industry was the government's role in research and development. Several research and experimental stations were owned and funded by the government. Their results were disseminated to the farming and horticultural industry and many of the solutions developed were applied widely on a field scale.

The government's intervention in the industry had its critics, but taken overall it was welcomed by the vast majority of farmers and horticulturalists. By any standards the government's contribution to the support of the industry was considerable and as a result British agriculture led the world. Output per man was well above that of other countries and efficiency was rated high.

It was argued later that it was a system which propped up the inefficient, and that grants and subsidies were used to keep in business units of production which were not viable. With all its faults, however, the policy succeeded in achieving two things. First, the population was well fed at what was then a reasonable cost, and secondly it produced high standards of farming at reasonable costs in all parts of the United Kingdom, from the East Anglian plains to the Highlands of Scotland and much in between.

Problems

The system of Government support did have its drawbacks, however, for today there are agricultural surpluses in Europe and the United Kingdom for which no market can be found. Some of the surpluses are used as aid to the starving people of other continents and some are sold at prices below cost. No one should complain that we are able to help the hungry with our surpluses, provided it is accepted that this is at a cost which should be shared by all sections of the community.

Although we were not aware of it at the time, this drive for maximum production brought other problems in its wake – perhaps the worst of which relates to the damage to the environment. One simple and telling example of this in East Anglia is that a high level of nitrogen used to increase crop yields over many years has led to serious pollution in the waterways where high levels of residual nitrogen are found. Alarm is spreading about other chemicals which have been used in the form of pesticides and herbicides. The full story is yet to be revealed, but many people are now questioning the use of these materials. Other problems are arising as a result of a policy of near mono-culture, practised in some areas. There are places where wheat is grown year after year without any apparent diminution of yield – but such yields are only obtained by the application of large amounts of fertilizers, and the use of protective chemicals against fungus disease and insect pests. It is believed that damage to the soil structure is taking place, which will take a long time to correct.

This account is not meant to be an indictment of the farmer, for he did not invent chemical fertilizers – they were introduced by scientists and were used under the guidance of the technocrats and the Ministry of Agriculture. This was genuinely thought to be the key to profitable farming and that unless they adopted it, the farmers would not survive in a highly competitive business.

So farming is now at a crossroads – with many doubts arising from all quarters. The government, alarmed at over-production, has introduced a scheme of grant payments aimed at taking land out of production. An acreage payment is made to farmers who are willing to take a proportion of their land out of production for a period, and further payments are made to assist the farmer who is willing to change the use of the land for recreational or conservation purposes. This is known as the 'Set Aside' scheme.

Back to the beginning

Positive encouragement is also being given to farmers in the form of advice to those who wish to pursue a system of extensive farming, sometimes known as 'organic farming'. The wheel has turned full circle for this is the system which was being practised in Lavenham in 1880 and up to the 1930s, by true husbandmen who did the job without subsidies or encouragement from Government because they knew it was the right thing to do. They were not 'muck and magic disciples' (to use a modern derogatory term for farmers who have turned against chemical fertilizers and sprays). They understood the soil with which they worked and they respected it. They were not in the business of maximum production, but were men who felt they had to leave the land in good heart for the generations which would follow. This attitude was adopted equally fervently by the farmworker who felt the same way about the land and the livestock with which he was in daily contact. In fact some farmworkers were more familiar with the land they worked than their boss for they walked it year in year out and saw the changes wrought by the seasons, and by the influence of crops and cultivations. They often had to decide when soil conditions were right for the job in hand, or when it was necessary to push ahead fast as a change in the weather became imminent.

It is difficult to summarise the essential elements involved in the system of husbandry being practised in Lavenham a hundred years ago, but ample evidence exists to enable us to look at the full picture.

There seems to be no doubt that the first principle in the mind of the farmer was respect for the soil – although he was often the owner of the land, he did not feel that he could do exactly as he wished with it. It was his responsibility to ensure that the fertility of the soil was maintained, and if he were a tenant, one of the conditions of his tenancy agreement was likely to have been that he would strive to maintain the land in 'good heart'. A good example of such a condition was that 'no hay should be sold off the farm'. Another might have been that 'a sound rotation of crops should be followed'. The underlying philosophy was that the land was the most important asset the farmer had and must be treated as such. In practice these conditions were not restrictive to the sound tenant, for unless they were honoured the value of the land asset would quickly fall.

Farming records

There are three contemporary records which demonstrate the soundness of the farming systems practised in Lavenham a hundred years

Building a stack at Hall Farm in the early 1900s

ago, and there are photographs of farm operations, albeit in some cases at a slightly later date. The farm diary of John Woodgate Baker is very significant, as is the notebook kept by his farm bailiff, Sam Fayers. These two documents form an authentic and revealing record of farming practices. In addition to these there is the newspaper report of a meeting of farmers in Lavenham in 1869 at the Swan Hotel, at which the subject of growing sugar beet was discussed.

Running through all these documents is the idea that the foundation of a sound system of good husbandry was a carefully worked out cropping plan. This was a very complex exercise for the farm had to be viewed as a whole and into such a plan had to be built the plan for the cropping of each individual field – not just for one year but for two or three years ahead. The key was that certain rules of crop rotation applied which would only be broken in exceptional circumstances.

The main crops grown were:

1 Wheat – mainly used for bread making, but some for cattle feed

2 Barley – for making beer and mainly sold to the maltsters
3 Oats for livestock feeding, especially horses
4 Turnips and mangolds – for sheep and cattle feeding throughout the winter
5 Beans and peas for livestock feeding
6 Red clover or trefoil – for cutting for hay
7 Permanent grassland

Other crops grown in Lavenham were carrots and sugar beet, but they were of minor importance. One golden rule in crop rotation, followed religiously, was that a crop of wheat should always follow a crop of beans or peas. This was because beans left a residual amount of nitrogen in the soil from which wheat in particular derived great benefit.

From 1892 John Woodgate Baker was farming Brights Farm, which was owned by the Baker family, and also Netherhall Farm of which he was then a tenant. In 1913 he bought both farms. The first entry in his farming diary was in 1903, and the amount of information recorded increased year by year.

The bailiff at Netherhall was Sam Fayers and in his notebook there is a record of the cropping plans from 1917 to 1928. It reveals how faithfully the principles of sound rotation of crops were carried out. It also demonstrates the other important principles which were followed in order to maintain a fertile, healthy and productive soil: regular generous dressings of farmyard manure, good drainage and control of weeds. In the latter case, fallowing the land at least once every ten years, and the growing of root crops which could be kept clean (weed free) by hoeing were the keys to success.

Sam Fayers' notebook shows us clearly what was going on at Netherhall, field by field during a period of 11 years, but the pattern emerges as we look in detail at the first five years.

The Five Acres (5 acres)
1917 Red Clover
1918 Wheat (Sulphate of ammonia 2 cwts)
1919 Barley (4 cwt per acre of manure)
1920 Trefoil
1921 Wheat*

* Red clover and trefoil (legumes) left residues of nitrogen useful to wheat growing.

Prentice Hill (9 acres)
1917 Oats
1918 Barley (2 cwts per acre bone Manure)
1919 Red Clover (Basic Slag 5 cwts)
1920 Wheat (Farm yard Manure)
1921 Barley (4 cwts per acre bone manure)

Prentice Hill (3 acres)
1917 Oats
1918 Barley (2 cwts per acre bone manure)
1919 Red Clover (Basic slag 5 cwts)
1920 Wheat (Farm Yard manure)
1921 Barley (4 cwts per acre bone manure)

Butt Field (8 acres)
1917 Red Clover (Basic Slag)
1918 Wheat (1 cwt per acre sulphate of amonia)
1919 Trefoil
1920 Winter Oats
1921 Trefoil (Self sown)*

Warrens Field (8 acres)
1917 Red Clover (Basic slag)
1918 Wheat (Farm Yard manure)
1919 Barley (Bone manure 4 cwts P.Acre)
1920 Trefoil
1921 Wheat

Great Woodfield (14 acres)
1917 Barley
1918 Winter Beans (Farmyard manure)
1919 Wheat.
1920 ½ Oats ½ Mangolds (F.Y.M)
1921 Barley.

Little Woodfield (6 acres)
1917 Barley
1918 Red Clover (Basic slag)
1919 Wheat
1920 Fallow
1921 Barley

* A second crop of trefoil grew from the seeds which had shed from the first crop.

Ploughing team at Milden near Lavenham, with manure heaps ready for spreading

Cutting wheat with a reaper at Hall Farm in the early 1900s

Gull Field (8 acres)
1917 Wheat
1918 Fallow
1919 Winter Beans (Farmyard Manure)
1921 Wheat.

Long Bridge (4 acres)
1917 Tares Fallow
1918 Oats
1919 Winter Beans (Farmyard manure)
1920 Wheat
1921 Long Fallow

Eight Acres (8 acres)
1917 Mangolds (Farmyard manure)
1918 Oats
1919 Red Clover (5 cwts Basic slag)
1920 Wheat Farmyard Manure)
1921 Winter Beans (4 cwts Basic Slag)

Home Field (9 acres)
1917 Peas (1 1/2 tons of yard manure per acre)
1918 Wheat (1 cwt per acre of Sulphate of ammonia)
1919 Mangolds (Farm Yard manure)
1920 Barley
1921 Peas.   (Sam Fayers, notebook, Lavenham Guildhall Museum)

These records (and those for a further seven years not quoted here) provide proof of a rigid adherence to the accepted rules of good husbandry and are in sharp contrast to the cropping plans of today, when often three or four straw crops are grown consecutively with no organic matter being incorporated into the soil. Some bag fertilizers were used, such as sulphate of ammonia and basic slag, but quantities were small compared with today.

In recent years grants have been paid to farmers who are willing to take land out of production for a period of time, but the process could hardly be called fallowing. In Sam Fayers' notebook there is a step by step account of how a field was fallowed.

Fifteen Acres (Fallow)
Ploughed   Dec 13th 1927
Ploughed back   March 28th 1928

Crossed	May 11th	"
2 horses harrowed	May 21st	"
Ploughed back	June 12th	"
Cultivated	June 23rd	"
Cultivated	July 3rd	"
Stetched up*	July 24th	"

So the golden rules of good husbandry were being followed at Nether-hall and most of the fields were receiving generous applications of farmyard manure. The rotation of crops was very sound and fallowing was a regular activity on the farm. In addition to his belief in sound husbandry Mr Baker contributed to the conservation of the environment by limiting the application of fertilizer. He played his full part in producing much needed food, both cereals and livestock. In the winter he kept his yards full of fattening cattle which were marketed at Bury St Edmunds and locally. Pigs from both farms were sold to the bacon factory or in the market at Bury. From time to time he sent poultry to the London markets and a steady flow of eggs left the farm for local shops.

As he was also involved in the family corn milling business in Prentice Street, much of his corn would be processed at the mill, some into flour, and some to be returned to the farm for cattle feed, but the diary record shows that a certain amount went on to the open market especially crops like peas and beans. In 1918 he sold peas at £4 2s 6d per coomb (4 bushels) and the yield from the crop was 11 coombs per acre. At the same time he sold seed beans at £5 per coomb. In the same year he states that he sold 2 Fat Sows at £29 each and that their live weight was nearly half a ton, (clearly the combined weight, but still pretty heavy). By the standards of the day the system practised by Mr Baker was highly productive.

In April 1869 a report appeared in the *Suffolk and Essex Free Press* which was highly significant. The writer was reporting on a meeting of the Lavenham Farmers' Club which had been held on the previous Tuesday evening. The following extracts demonstrate what a high

---

* This was a local term for ridged. In this case the operation was probably done to prepare for a particular crop, for drilling on the top of ridges was common. This was a very thorough process and of course costly. Today's answer would be to control the weeds by using chemical herbicides which are not cheap and in some cases dangerous if handled incorrectly.

Mr Mortlock's threshing engine in operation

level of technical expertise in crop production was being achieved by the farmers of Lavenham and district at that time.

In the unavoidable absence of G. Mumford Esq. who has lately suffered severely from the effects of an accident, Mr T. P. Hitchcock was voted into the chair, and there were also present the following gentlemen – Messrs. Biddell, Fish, J. E. Wright, R. Edgar, W. B. Hustler, R. Hawkins (Milden) and two sons, W. Making, C. S. Scott, F. J. Barkway, Thomas J. King, S. Blomfield, T. Hitchcock, jun., E. Hitchcock, Makin, Thos. Baker, Mothersole, Sach, Vince (2), R. Woodgate, Jackson, Smith, W. Barber (Secretary). Etc.

The chairman . . . announced the subject for the evening's discussion to be as to the growth of beet root for sugar, a subject with which he had no doubt all present were well acquainted . . . Mr Hawkins read a paper which was as follows:

'Having been requested to suggest a subject for discussion . . . I ventured to suggest that of the cultivation of beet root, that being, I believe, a root more suitable to a heavy land district, and ought to be a remunerative crop for farmers to grow. [At about this time a sugar beet factory had been built in Lavenham and many farmers had started to grow the beet root for supplying to the factory] . . . The business of the farmer, as far as regards the production of crops, consists in knowing what elements any given crop will require and in taking care that a due supply of these elements in a mineral state, and also in such alliances as are soluble in water, be present in the soil. Nearly two thousand years ago, Cato said one of the most important rules of husbandry was 'bene arare', or, in plain English, to plough well; and good ploughing is still essential to the profitable cultivation of the soil. The action of ordinary ploughing is that it exposes the elements forming the soil, and particularly the humus, to air and moisture, by the action of which they form combinations that are soluble in water . . .

'Farmyard manure is efficacious just because it restores to the soil those very elements that were previously abstracted from it. I presume the increase in fertility of land upon which guano [long accumulated dung of sea birds generally imported from South America] is spread is owing to the guano containing all elements which ordinary crops require, with the exception of potassium salt. Bone dust gives the land phosphate of lime; nitrate of soda gives nitrogen and soda; sulphate of ammonia gives sulphur and nitrogen . . . Lime likewise acts by its abstraction of water of undecomposed vegetable matter, and thereby promoting its putrefaction.

'It is plain that many practical rules held in esteem by the majority of the agricultural world are not compatible with the views of science. For example, two white straw crops in succession, or in any manner exhausting the soil, is held to be bad farming, and frequently prohibited in leases . . . but now that the action of the soil upon the plant is known, it would appear that prohibitions of cropping and compulsory rotations of crops are inexpedient. It is not taking too much out of the land that is to be avoided, but it is the putting plenty back that must be insisted on.

'. . . My usual plan for growing beet root has been after a wheat crop, that crop having been previously dressed with about 12 loads per acre of good farmyard manure. If the land is clean I rarely plough more than once for mangolds, and as early as possible after harvest . . . varying between 5 and 8 inches deep as the soil admits . . . I usually apply in the spring . . . 2 cwt. of guano and 2 cwt. of salt per acre . . . harrowing the land after with the Clabon or duckfoot harrow twice over.'

He considered that the growth of sugar beet was very widely different to the growth of the common beet; and that if they grow successfully they must make some arrangement in the district by which they might obtain a sub soil plough. (from a transcription of a report in the *Suffolk and Essex Free Press*, 1st April 1869, Lavenham Guildhall Museum)

This report gives us an insight into the high level of knowledge amongst farmers about the properties of the soil they farmed. Here again attention to detail was clearly in the front of their minds, along with the overriding need to ensure that soil was kept in good heart.

These records illustrate amongst other things that the systems demanded a large labour force by comparison with the situation today. The gradual introduction of mechanization set in train a flow of labour away from the land, until today an absolute minimum has been reached. The substitution of capital for labour has not been all gain. Many highly skilled men have over the years had to leave their employment on the land, and in many cases reluctantly. In doing so they have been unable to find job satisfaction. It is true to say, however, that ex-farmworkers have adapted well to their new working environment, often to the advantage of their new employers.

Old answers to modern problems
With farming in the United Kingdom at present facing a crisis, it may be sensible to look back over these hundred years and see if there are lessons to be learned which may help to solve some of the present problems. I am not suggesting that we turn back the clock, for that would be nonsense. On the other hand does it make any sense to take our most valuable asset, land, and pay farmers for not using it? Why not adopt a more enlightened system of crop rotation and bring back the system of fallowing to control our weed population, thus gradually reducing our reliance on heavy doses of pesticides with their attendant dangers? Why not once more go back to the system of yarding cattle through the winter – which is in fact happening on some Lavenham farms – thereby having available large supplies of farmyard manure for returning to the land? The means are available for moving such materials at low cost. More people would be needed on farms and in the present situation of high unemployment this would be a benefit.

Knowing as we do that unless we change our ways and face up to the dangers which threaten our environment, succeeding generations will pay a heavy price, we need to examine any idea which might contribute to solving some of the acute problems which beset us. The pattern of farming in Lavenham and many other places a hundred years ago might serve as a starting point in our quest for solutions to problems. This must be one of the purposes of the study of history.

7 People who influenced events in Lavenham

Throughout the ages all communities have felt the influence of certain members of their community. Such influence may not always have been for the good, although the person concerned may well have thought that it was. Frequently the individual may have been totally unaware that they had been exercising influence, for the results of their work might have been long delayed before they were perceived as benefits. In some cases the work of an individual may stand as a reminder of the person, long after their life has ended, for the quality of the work stands out as something which other people may strive to emulate.

Making assessments about the influence of individuals is a somewhat subjective exercise, but often there is a consensus amongst the community which points in the right direction. No one category of person has a monopoly of power to influence others. Wealth, authority, intellect, age or experience may not necessarily bestow on an individual the power to influence. Many remain totally unaware that they have influenced anyone. This chapter confines itself to people in Lavenham who were involved in farming and about whom some information is available. There were no doubt others who merit inclusion, but on whom I have no information.

William Biddell

No account of farming in Lavenham would be complete without reference to William Biddell, Member of Parliament, Justice of the Peace. He was a man of many parts, large in his appearance, and large in his achievements. He moved to Lavenham in 1868 on marrying Mary Ann Scott, having lost his first wife. Mrs Scott inherited Lavenham Hall and estate from her father, Robert Howard, and it was here that William Biddell began a most energetic and varied chapter in his life. A story is told in connection with his weight, that on a visit to Lavenham station

William Biddell

he enquired of the stationmaster how much his set of scales would weigh. 'Twenty stones Sir' was the reply. 'We'll put it to the test' said William Biddell, and sure enough, when he stepped on there was a loud clang, indicating that the maximum weight had easily registered.

William Biddell's primary interest was the mangement of the farm at Lavenham Hall, and in addition managing the other farms which he bought, Priory Farm, Glebe Farm and Frogs Hall Farm.

In 1880 William Biddell was elected MP for West Suffolk. He had previously sought nomination for the seat but had been unsuccessful because at the time he was not a landowner. He was the first MP to be elected with a background of tenant farming. It seems clear that his knowledge of farming was a considerable asset in the House of Commons and there was an occasion when he chartered a special train to London so that he could be present in the House in the division lobby when a vote was called for.

When Parliament was dissolved in 1884 he did not seek re-election; this was a deliberate decision arising out of a situation in which he had been involved. The workers at the horsehair factory at Glemsford were on strike. A meeting was convened between the employers and the workers at the Bull Hotel in Long Melford. He had been invited to mediate in the dispute. The men had walked from Glemsford on a very cold, wet night and were in an angry mood. William Biddell took the side of the employers, but it appears that afterwards he felt he had misjudged the situation. As a consequence of this he felt that he should not seek re-election to Parliament.

Giving up his seat in Parliament no doubt gave him more time to devote to the affairs of Lavenham and Suffolk; for he was involved in many activities. He was an auctioneer and valuer as well as a land agent. He owned a small auction market near the station where cattle and pigs were sold as well as dead stock. He also conducted auction sales of farms as well as commercial and residential property throughout Suffolk, as a partner in the firm of Biddell and Blencowe, who were the biggest firm of auctioneers and land agents in the county at that time.

He was at one time President of the Suffolk Society of Agricultural Valuers of which he was a founder member; this was established in 1848 and was the first of its kind in the country. William Biddell's membership stretched over a period of 50 years and it was claimed that he never missed a meeting. He was a County Councillor, a Justice of the Peace and a member of the governing body of the Lavenham County School, all posts in which he took a keen interest.

William Biddell died in 1900 leaving a daughter, Bertha, who inherited the estate. Bertha's marriage to the Reverend Henry Taylor had taken place only a few months before her father died. The funeral service took place in Lavenham church and a large number of people attended to pay their tributes. The cortège moved in procession to the parish chuch of Hawstead for the burial ceremony. Many people followed on foot, and the horses drawing the hearse were all decked in black. As the procession neared the village the people of Hawstead had walked out to meet it and join it on its way to the church.

The lychgate at Hawstead church was erected by Mrs Biddell in memory of her husband, and in Lavenham church a memorial tablet is to be found in the Lady Chapel. He was churchwarden there for many years. A quotation on his memorial reads 'The memory of the just is blessed' (Proverbs x. 7.); this would seem to have been a fitting reflection of his life. In his will he left a bequest for gifts of coal to the poor of Lavenham, and for the upkeep of the church. Coals for the poor at this time would have been a most welcome gift for those –

and there were many – trying to live on very slender means. There is no doubt that William Biddell contributed much to the life of Lavenham, first as an employer, and in many other ways.

John Woodgate Baker
A lot has already been said about John Woodgate Baker as a practising farmer but he was also involved in the family corn milling business. The farms and the mill together were a source of sound employment over a long period, and it must follow that his ability to manage all these enterprises and keep men in employment was a most worthy achievement in itself. The same can be said about his father, Thomas Baker, who took a bold initiative in developing the steam mill in Lavenham, which proved to be a great boon to the prosperity of the village. He was also responsible for running the maltings in Lady Street for many years.

Bertram Death
Although it is true that farmers needed men to carry out their work, it is equally true that the men needed the farmers to secure their livelihood. There was one farmer in particular, Bertram Death, of whom it was said that if he came to the village and saw a man idle on the street, he would tell him to report to Balsdon Hall Farm or Slough Farm where a job would be found for him. Mr Death was farming at Balsdon Hall Farm, just over the parish boundary, and also in 1919 at Slough Farm when he took over the tenancy. He ultimately bought Slough Farm from Sir William Hyde Parker who owned the Melford Park Estate.

Mr Death owned a number of threshing machines and no doubt some of the extra men he employed would travel round the farms with these. The fact that he found employment for so many men who badly needed work marks him out as one who contributed very positively to the life of the village. He was also very much involved in the affairs of the village.

Bertha and Henry Taylor
For seven years after the death of her father Bertha Taylor lived at Lavenham Hall and ran the estate with the help of her husband. He was the curate at Lavenham and took a great interest in the farms and

the estate as well as carrying out his duties in the parish. In 1907 Henry Taylor was appointed rector of the parish of Great Barton, Suffolk. He had a great desire to become the rector of Lavenham, but because his wife was the major landowner in the parish such an appointment was thought inappropriate by the church authorities. They took up residence in Great Barton. Lavenham Hall was then let to Cordy S. Wolton, a highly respected and successful farmer from Ixworth in Suffolk where his family had farmed for many years.

In 1914 Henry Taylor contracted an illness and was advised to enter hospital for treatment. He refused to go, on the grounds that the beds should be reserved for wounded servicemen returning from France, and as he did not get the appropriate treatment his condition deteriorated and he died. Bertha Taylor moved to Bradfield Combust with her family until Cordy Wolton retired in 1927 when she returned to her birthplace at Lavenham Hall, remaining there until her death in 1955. Bertha Taylor had a great affection for the village and was highly respected by the people. She had many gifts, including painting in watercolours.

Bertha Taylor's eldest daughter Mollie married Mr H. C. Wolton of Bury St Edmunds, (a member of the Wolton family of Ixworth) who was a well-known land agent and valuer and who acted for Mrs Taylor's executors in the sale of the Lavenham Estate, following her death.

Cordy Wolton

Cordy Wolton farmed at Lavenham Hall from 1907 and in addition to running a successful farming business there, founded the Lavenham Stud of Suffolk Punch horses, from stock bred by his father at Ixworth. The stud came to be recognized as one of the best in the county and achieved national recognition. Horses from the stud frequently won awards at the Suffolk Show. At its peak there were 34 horses at the stud, and when it was dispersed in 1927 one of the horses sold at 1,300 guineas.

Fred Huffey

There were many craftsmen working in Lavenham a hundred years ago as we have already seen. Many of them ran highly successful businesses and provided services of a high standard, and many of them were household names. The name of Fred Huffey stands out amongst them. His forge in Water Street was like a magnet, especially to the young people. The glow of the forge and the ring of the anvil spelt action, excitement and, no doubt, often welcome warmth. Fred Huffey was a highly qualified blacksmith and with his two sons he brought great skill and energy to the craft. As the main blacksmith in the village over a period of fifty years, he was respected and admired not only for his skills but for his qualites as a man. Many who visited his forge with their horses would surely have been influenced by his personality, and much of his work in wrought iron can still be seen in the village. He was much in demand when medieval buildings were being restored. Many of the oak doors are hung on wrought iron hinges fashioned by him along with much of the door furniture. He produced handrails in character, for many of the houses were entered by steps. In these and many other ways he left his indelible mark on the life of Lavenham.

Sam Fayers

In chapter 5 is an account of the contribution of farmworkers to the community. In such groups of men some would emerge as leaders, and as such would be selected to take on extra resposibility by their employers. One such man was Sam Fayers, who was farm bailiff to John Woodgate Baker when he was farming at Brights and Nether Hall farms. Sam Fayers would be responsible for the day-to-day management of the farms under the direction of Mr Baker. He would be given a cropping plan by Mr Baker and from then on he would have to ensure that the plan was carried out. On a daily basis he would allocate jobs to the farm staff, checking that horses and carts were available, and where used, machinery was available. He would have to decide when operations had to be carried out and make sure that supplies of seed, *et cetera*, were ready to hand. His responsibilities were quite extensive and he would have to supervise the men who looked after the livestock. He was in fact a master craftsman and manager rolled into one, and highly valued for his knowledge and skill. The evidence of his responsibility and ability appears in his record books, which are quoted in chapter 6. They are presented in a very neat and tidy form, with great attention to detail. Sam Fayers exemplified a person who influenced agricultural events in Lavenham.

William Faiers, the head horseman at Hall Farm. Behind him is the fruits of a year's work, a full stackyard

William Faiers

Another key workman was the head horseman. The head horseman at Lavenham Hall Farm, William Faiers, was a man of many skills in addition to his overriding responsibility for the horses. He would be taken into consultation with the farm foreman or bailiff when decisions had to be made about operations on the land. He would know every field because he walked them daily following his horses. Respected by his employer and by his fellow workers because of his high level of skill and strength of character, he was known as a 'gentle' man – an attribute which undoubtedly accounted for his success with horses. Clearly a man who influenced events.

William W. Roper

Lavenham escaped some of the worst hardships of a hundred years ago because of the industrial development which took place from about 1850 onwards until 1930. One man must be given much of the credit for the enterprise he showed in furthering such developments. William W Roper was the son-in-law of the originator of the development, John Churchyard. William Roper became the owner of the business and in addition to expanding the production of horse hair

William Roper (centre) poses with his family

fabric, he started the manufacture of coconut matting. The big expansion in both these enterprises took place between 1864 and 1900. At one time 203 people were employed in horsehair fabric production and many of these were daughters or wives of agricultural workers. The same applied to the making of coconut matting where several farmworker's sons were found work.

William Roper built many first-class houses in the village for the workers in his factories. These, mostly built of red brick, stand today as a memorial to his drive and enterprise. Many of them carry his name and the date they were built.

The foregoing list of people is undoubtedly incomplete, for there were many more whose influence must have been considerable, but whose names are not recorded for posterity in the annals of Lavenham farming. There are many also whose activities were not directly related to agriculture. Their stories can be found elsewhere, all worthy of exploration.

Since that time a hundred years ago until now a list could be compiled of people who influenced events in Lavenham. Such a list would be long and many interesting facts would come to light – but that is another slice of Lavenham's history.